...OL. 64
...O INCLUDES U.S. NAVY
...4Y-1 & PB4Y-2 VERSIONS

B-24
LIBERATOR

in detail

Bert Kinzey

 squadron/signal publications

COPYRIGHT © 2000 BY DETAIL & SCALE, INC.

This book is a product of Detail & Scale, Inc., which has sole responsibility for its content and layout, except that all contributors are responsible for the security clearance and copyright release of all materials submitted. Published by Squadron/Signal Publications, 1115 Crowley Drive, Carrollton, Texas 75011.

CONTRIBUTORS AND SOURCES:

Al Lloyd	Jim Roeder	Jim Galloway
Stan Piet	Bill Slatton	National Archives
Lloyd Jones	Bob Bartolacci	United States Air Force Museum
Larry Webster	Stan Parker	National Museum of Naval Aviation

The author and Detail & Scale, Inc. express a sincere word of thanks to Bob Spaulding and his volunteers at the United States Air Force Museum for their invaluable assistance and for allowing the author to take detailed photographs throughout the interior of the B-24D Liberator on display at the museum. Appreciation is also extended to David Menard in the museum's research division for his help during the development of this book.

Special appreciation is also expressed to Al Lloyd, who provided many of the black and white photographs for this publication, and to Stan Piet, who contributed the vintage color photographs.

For the most complete coverage of the B-24's development and operational history, we recommend, Liberator, America's Global Bomber, by Alwyn T. Lloyd. This 548-page volume is the best reference available on the B-24's record in World War II and during the years that immediately followed. The book was originally released in 1993, and plans call for it to be republished in 2000.

Many photographs in this publication are credited to their contributors. Photographs with no credit indicated were taken by the author.

ISBN 1-888974-17-6

Above left, front cover photo: "Joisey Bounce" flies lead for three other Liberators of the 93rd Bomb Group. This B-24D, 41-24226, was formerly named "Utah Man," and it was a survivor of the famous raid against Ploesti on August 1, 1943. The Liberator next to "Joisey Bounce" is "The Dutchess," and this B-24D, 41-24147, also participated in the Ploesti mission. (Piet collection)

Above right, rear cover, top photo: A sinister dragon's face appears on a Liberator of the 308th Bomb Group. This was a B-24D that had a Consolidated A-6 turret fitted to its nose at a field depot. (Piet collection)

Right, rear cover, bottom photo: Details and colors of the R-1830 powerplants are visible in this vintage World War II photograph taken while ground crew personnel performed maintenance on a B-24E. (Piet collection)

INTRODUCTION

The silhouette of the B-24 was very distinctive from every angle. Notice how the left landing gear has lagged behind the right during the retraction sequence and is not yet fully inside the gear well between the two engines on the left wing. **(National Archives)**

During World War II, the U. S. Army Air Forces used three different heavy bombers in large numbers. They included the B-17 Flying Fortress, the B-24 Liberator, and the B-29 Superfortress, and of these, the B-24 received considerably less acclaim than the other two. Although it became operational late in the war, the B-29 made its indelible mark in history when Superfortresses dropped the two atomic bombs on Japan. With its unusual design, pressurized crew areas, remotely sighted gun turrets, and other innovations, the Superfortress was a generation beyond the B-17 and B-24 in bomber development. It was also used only in the Pacific against the Japanese. But the Flying Fortress and the Liberator were true contemporaries. Both were developed in the years immediately prior to America's entry into World War II, and both were operational in all theaters throughout the war until the Japanese surrendered in September 1945.

Several of Boeing's B-17s were in the news the day the Japanese attacked Pearl Harbor when a flight of Flying Fortresses approached the Hawaiian Islands that Sunday morning of December 7, 1941. The bombers arrived over Hickham Field at the same time the Japanese attacked, thus beginning the war unarmed and out of gas. From that day forward, the B-17 Flying Fortress seemed to gain far greater fame and recognition than its counterpart, the B-24 Liberator. More than fifty years after the war, the B-17 remains the best known of the three U. S. heavy bombers of the war.

Although the B-17 was an excellent design, and it performed magnificently throughout the war, the fact that it is much better known than the B-24 seems difficult to understand. This is also unfair to both the aircraft itself and the crews who maintained and flew it. Perhaps part of the reason for this disparity can be attributed to the fact that the B-17 was used more extensively in England where the majority of the U. S. media covered the

war. Because of this, the Flying Fortress received more attention and was photographed more often than the Liberator. But when one bomber is compared to the other, the B-24 was the superior aircraft in many important categories. It could carry a heavier load over a greater range than the B-17, and it was used more extensively from a geographical point of view. The Liberator was also built in greater numbers than the Flying Fortress. In fact, more B-24s were built than any other American aircraft in history.

The B-24 Liberator was also one of the most modified aircraft in military history. Including the Navy's PB4Y-2 Privateer, no less than ten different versions were produced, and these had numerous variations depending on which version was involved, where they were built, and where they may have been modified in the field. The design of the bomb aiming windows, and even how the anti-glare panel was painted on natural metal aircraft, varied even on the same version of the Liberator depending on who built the particular aircraft involved. Therefore, a complete accounting of every change and modification is not possible since many probably were never conclusively documented. But even a reference that is reasonably complete in covering all aspects of the Liberator is not possible in an 80 page book like this one.

The focus of this "In Detail" volume will be on the physical details of the B-24 and PB4Y. Although it is impossible to illustrate every modification ever made to these aircraft, we have concentrated on showing the important common details more extensively than any previous publication. Using the B-24D as a basis, we have illustrated the details of the cockpit and other interior compartments, the armament, landing gear, powerplant, wings, and tail section. Changes made from one version to the next are shown with the appropriate variants to which they apply. Likewise, we have illustrated the details of the PB4Y-2 Privateer, concentrating mainly on the interior which has rarely been included in previous references.

Concluding the book is our usual Modelers Summary which takes a look at the model kits of the Liberator and Privateer available to the scale modeler. Recommendations are made as to which are the best in each scale.

DEVELOPMENTAL HISTORY

Consolidated's Model 31 flying boat, designated the XP4Y-1 by the Navy, was the first aircraft to fly with the Davis wing. It also had the oval-shaped twin tail design and other features that were carried forward to Model 32 which became the B-24 Liberator. *(Jones collection)*

In the mid-1930s, most of the leadership in the U. S. Army still thought of the airplane as a tactical weapon to be used in support of the forces on the ground. Little if any thought was given to developing long range bombers that could strike deep into the enemy's homeland to reduce his ability to make war. At least part of the reason that little consideration had been given to such strategic use of aircraft was because aircraft development had not progressed enough for a truly effective long range bomber to be designed and produced. As a result, existing bombers, like the Douglas B-18, were usually twin-engine tactical designs, and their primary mission was to fly in direct support of the ground army.

By the late 1937, aeronautical engineering, powerplant development, and other systems had progressed to the point where a long range bomber could be developed. Fortunately, a few leaders in the U. S. Army had the foresight to see the value of such an aircraft in future conflicts. Among these was General Henry "Hap" Arnold, but he fought an uphill battle convincing the War Department of the need for such an aircraft. In 1938, President Franklin D. Roosevelt's call for an expanded military aircraft production program helped Arnold convince the War Department to fund America's first strategic bomber, and as a result, the Boeing B-17 Flying Fortress was designed and put into production. But Arnold wanted a second bomber as well, and Consolidated was ready with a proposal for a long range bomber that it claimed would outperform the B-17.

The choice of Consolidated as the company to design and build the new bomber was a bit curious, because until that time, it had been primarily involved in building flying boats for the Navy. Of these, the PBY Catalina was to become the most famous as it served admirably throughout World War II and for several years thereafter.

At the time Consolidated began work on the new strategic bomber, it was working on the development of the XP4Y flying boat. Known as Model 31 at Consolidated, this aircraft was the first to fly with the highly efficient Davis wing design that offered better lift and additional range through reduced drag when compared to standard airfoils. Model 31 also had a twin vertical tail design, and both of these features, along with several others, would be used on Model 32, Consolidated's designation for its proposed strategic bomber.

Another feature of the Model 32 was a tricycle landing gear that would shorten the takeoff roll. This would make the B-24 the first production bomber to have the tricycle landing gear arrangement. Slots were cut into the leading edge of the wing, but these proved unsatisfactory, and they were deleted on subsequent versions.

After reviewing the design, the Army placed an order for a single XB-24 on March 30, 1939, and the aircraft made its first flight only nine months later on December 29, 1939. It was soon flown from California to Wright Field, Ohio, where it continued its flight testing. Meanwhile, an order was placed for seven YB-24 service test aircraft. However, of the seven YB-24s ordered, only the seventh was completed as a YB-24, while the first six were delivered as early B-24Ds. Six other aircraft were also completed to basically the same standards as the YB-24 and were provided to the British for use as long range transports. They were called LB-30As by the RAF.

Although the Army was impressed with the aircraft,

The design of the Liberator was firmly established on the sole XB-24. The nose section would be lengthened, and armament changes would be made, but otherwise, no major changes were made to the basic design throughout the entire production run. (National Archives)

it was France that placed the first order in June 1940. But before the order could be filled, France fell to the Germans. As a result, the first twenty aircraft in the order were provided to the RAF as LB-30Bs, and nine were designated B-24As and acquired by the U. S. Army for testing. They were subsequently redesignated RB-24As and used by the U. S. Army Ferry Command as long range transports. The remaining aircraft in the French order were completed as B-24Cs and B-24Ds.

Much erroneous information has been published concerning how the name Liberator was bestowed on the aircraft. Some accounts state that it was the British who gave it this name, while others say that Ruben Fleet of Consolidated named the bomber. But the evidence clearly indicates that the name was chosen by Consolidated's employees.

The LB-30As were the first examples of the design to enter service with the British, but being considered unworthy for combat, they were used only as transports over the North Atlantic ferry routes. The first to see combat were the twenty Liberator Is used by the RAF's

Coastal Command in the war against German U-boats. These were followed by Liberator IIs in British service.

After only nine B-24Cs were completed, the B-24D became the first version to be built in large numbers. It would be this version that would be the first to see extensive action with the USAAF in the heavy bomber role for which it was conceived. By the end of 1943, Liberators were in action in every theater of the war, and it gained the most fame and recognition during Operation Tidal Wave, flying against the oil refineries at Ploesti, Rumania. Most noteworthy of these raids was the low level mission flown on August 1, 1943.

To produce the large numbers of aircraft needed for the war effort, a production pool was developed where manufacturers built aircraft designed by other companies, and companies previously engaged in other production during peacetime set up assembly lines to build aircraft. In the case of the Liberator, many were built at Consolidated's plants at San Diego, California, and Fort Worth, Texas. North American Aviation, busily building its own P-51 Mustangs, B-25 Mitchells, and other aircraft, used plant space in Dallas, Texas, to build B-24s as well, and Douglas Aircraft built Liberators in Tulsa, Oklahoma. The Ford Motor Company operated the fifth production line, building Liberators in a huge new plant in Willow Run, Michigan, near Detroit. Although the Fort Worth and Tulsa plants primarily produced sub-assemblies that were completed at the other facilities, they also delivered some

The B-24D was the first variant of the Liberator to be produced in large numbers. It was this version that was used on the famous raid against Ploesti on August 1, 1943. (National Archives)

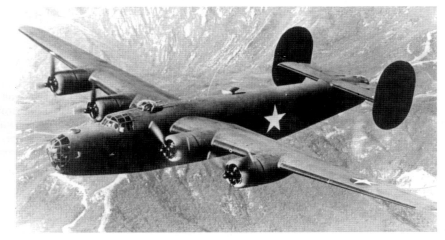

The B-24G was the first version to be fitted with a nose turret as a production standard. *(Lloyd collection)*

complete aircraft as well. The following chart summarizes the Liberator production pool:

COMPANY	PLANT LOCATION	SUFFIX*
Consolidated	San Diego	CO
Consolidated	Fort Worth	CF
Douglas Aircraft	Tulsa	DT
North American Aviation	Dallas	NT
Ford Motor Company	Willow Run	FO

* These two letters were used as a suffix in the full designation of the aircraft to distinguish where it was built. For example, a B-24D-125-CO would be a B-24D of production block 125 built by Consolidated at San Diego.

The British had proven that the Liberator was the best aircraft in the world for long range maritime patrol missions, and ever increasing numbers were added to the squadrons of the Coastal Command throughout the war. The U. S. Army also began using the B-24D in this role, but the mission was eventually turned over to the U. S. Navy. The Navy began acquiring stock B-24Ds which it redesignated PB4Y-1s, and these aircraft were used extensively for the long range patrol missions around America's coastlines. But the Navy wanted an aircraft optimized for this role, and it was the adaptability of the Liberator's design that led to the highly modified PB4Y-2 Privateer. Some of these aircraft would remain in service for twenty years before finally being replaced by the Lockheed P-3 Orion in the 1960s.

The sound design of Consolidated's Model 32 is illustrated by the fact that it remained basically unchanged throughout all of the production variants except the PB4Y-2. The only modifications of any real consequence involved improvements to the defensive armament, and most noticeable of these was the addition of a power operated nose turret beginning with the twenty-sixth B-24G. Waist windows were also enclosed on later variants for crew comfort. Otherwise, external differ-

ences were limited to redesigned nose gear doors, a different arrangement for the wing tip navigation lights, improved deicing equipment, and the constantly changing design and arrangement of the various scanning windows.

The B-24 is often compared to its contemporary, the B-17 Flying Fortress. The B-24 could carry a heavier payload over a longer range than the B-17, and it had a marginally better lost rate in combat than the Flying Fortress. On the negative side, the Liberator was more difficult to fly, and it was particularly hard to hold in tight box formations above 20,000 feet. Another liability was directly connected with the Davis wing design. As efficient as the wing was, its narrow chord made it far less survivable than a wing with a broader chord like that found on the B-17. Battle damage to any major structural component of the Davis wing almost always resulted in the wing folding back along the side of the fuselage and the loss of the aircraft and crew. However, in the fuselage and tail structures, the Liberator could sustain as much damage as the Flying Fortress. Although arguments for and against both aircraft can be made when discussing the bomber role, the Liberator and Privateer were clearly the best long range maritime patrol aircraft in the service of any nation during World War II and for many years thereafter.

Liberators were used in large numbers by the Royal Air Force, both as a conventional bomber and a long range patrol aircraft. The Liberator squadrons of the Coastal Command played a critical role in winning the Battle of the Atlantic against German U-boats. (Lloyd collection)

Cargo and tanker versions of the Liberator provided long range logistics support for the USAAF. This is a C-109 Liberator Express transport aircraft. It could carry up to twenty-five passengers or 12,000 pounds of cargo. (Lloyd collection)

The Liberator's design also proved far more adaptable than that of the Flying Fortress, and this was primarily due to the larger and more spacious fuselage. Primary among the derivatives were the C-87 Liberator Express and RY-3 transport aircraft as well as the C-109 fuel tanker. But many other Liberators were modified after delivery for special operations and missions. Some were crammed full of special radar and other electronics gear, while others had extensive radio equipment installed.

Although the U. S. Army Air Force was the primary user of the Liberator, many other countries also flew B-24s and PB4Ys during and after World War II. The Royal Air Force was second only to the United States in the number of Liberators used in operational service. The British utilized it primarily as a long range patrol aircraft, and twenty-two squadrons of the Coastal Command were equipped with various marks of the Liberator. After the war, the British Ministry of Defense went on record as stating that these squadrons made the difference in winning the Battle of the Atlantic.

Sixteen squadrons of Bomber Command also operated Liberators, but these were only used in overseas areas, because the British considered the Liberator less suitable for European operations than its own Lancaster bomber. Within the British Commonwealth, six squadrons of the Royal Canadian Air Force, two of the South African Air Force, and nine of the Royal Australian Air Force were equipped with Liberators at some time during World War II. Number 321 Squadron in the RAF was manned by crews from the Dutch East Indies.

In the post-war years, refurbished B-24Js were flown by the Indian Air Force for maritime patrol missions, while the French acquired PB4Y-1s and PB4Y-2s for use in Indochina. The Nationalist Chinese Air Force flew ten Liberators for a short time in 1944, and after the war it acquired thirty-seven B-24Ms. In 1952, Nationalist China also received thirty-eight PB4Y-2s.

The B-24 Liberator was America's first aircraft to enter mass production, and a total of 18,188 were built, counting all versions. This is the largest number of any American aircraft ever built. It is a record the Liberator is likely to hold forever.

In retrospect, America's decision to design, develop, and produce long range strategic bombers played an important part in the ultimate victory in World War II. Great Britain was the only other nation in the war to deploy strategic bombers in large numbers. In contrast, Germany and Japan relied almost entirely on twin-engine tactical bombers, and many historians believe that the war in Europe would have been very different if the Luftwaffe had developed and deployed large numbers of heavy bombers. Fortunately, only the Americans and the British possessed the capabilities provided by these big strategic bombers, and they contributed significantly to the final outcome of the war. In every theater, the B-24 Liberator was there to make a major contribution.

The final production variant of the Liberator series of aircraft was the much modified Navy PB4Y-2 Privateer. It was optimized for long range patrol missions at low altitudes. (NMNA)

LIBERATOR VARIANTS
XB-24 & XB-24B

A flying view of the XB-24B shows the spinners on the propeller hubs and the red, white, and blue markings on the tails. In this later photograph, the pitot probes are on the nose.

(Jones collection)

Consolidated developed the design for its Model 32 during early 1939, and after it was reviewed by the Army, a production contract for a single XB-24, serial number 39-556, was issued on March 30 of that year. Less than nine months later, the aircraft was rolled out, and Consolidated's chief test pilot, Bill Wheatley, was at the controls when the XB-24 took off on its maiden flight on December 29, 1939.

As originally built, the inner wing structure was designed to be a fuel tank, and this was known as a wet wing. Four Pratt & Whitney R-1830-33 engines with

mechanical two-speed superchargers were initially installed in the XB-24.

In early 1940, the aircraft was flown to Wright Field, Ohio, for extensive tests and evaluation. The aircraft was modified and improved over the next several months, and it was officially accepted by the USAAC on August 13, 1940.

The R-1830-33 powerplants were first replaced with R-1830-41s with General Electric B-2 turbosuperchargers, and later, turbosupercharged R-1830-43s were installed. Spinners were added to the propeller hubs, and self-sealing fuel bladders were fitted into the wings. This reduced fuel capacity by a small margin, but the U. S. Army believed they were necessary for a combat aircraft. With these improvements, the aircraft was redesignated the XB-24B, and it first flew in this new configuration on February 1, 1941.

An earlier photograph of the XB-24 illustrates that the spinners were not initially on the propeller hubs. Also note the pitot probe in its original location on the leading edge of the right wing. Although they are very difficult to see in this photograph, there were slots under the leading edge of the wings of the XB-24, but these were deleted on the subsequent YB-24 and all later versions of the Liberator.

(Lloyd collection)

YB-24 & LB-30A

The U. S. Army Air Corps ordered seven YB-24s, serial numbers 40-696 through 40-702 which were very similar to the XB-24B except that the slots in the leading edge of the wings were deleted. Deicer boots were added to the leading edge of the wings and tail surfaces. Only the last of the seven aircraft, serial number 40-702, was actually completed as a YB-24. The first six, serial numbers 40-696 through 40-701, were completed to early B-24D standards. The single YB-24 was used for flight testing, and it was eventually retained for use by Consolidated. It was redesignated the RB-24 with the R standing for restricted.

Great Britain received six LB-30As that were basically completed to the same standards as the YB-24, except that the Royal Air Force specified that they would have .303-caliber machine guns for defensive armament instead of the .50-caliber weapons preferred by the U. S. Army. However, they were not considered ready for combat, so these six aircraft were used by the British as transports across the North Atlantic ferry routes.

It should be noted that some confusion exists between the six LB-30As and the six YB-24s that were completed to early B-24D standards for the U. S. Army. Some references state that these were the same six aircraft, but this is not the case. Although all seven YB-24s, including the six delivered as B-24Ds, and the six LB-30As were all completed from airframes from the original French order, the LB-30As were not the same six aircraft as the YB-24s that became the first B-24Ds.

Seven YB-24s were ordered, but six were delivered as B-24Ds. The one airframe that was completed as a YB-24, 40-702, was used for flight tests, and it was eventually retained by Consolidated. It had the short nose as found on the XB-24, but it was painted in the Olive Drab over Neutral Gray scheme. *(National Archives)*

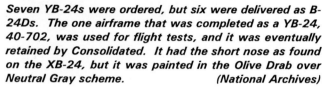

The YB-24 had flat disc plates behind the propeller hubs during part of its flight testing, but these were not always present. Browning .50-caliber machine guns were specified as the defensive armament. *(USAFM)*

Six LB-30As were completed to essentially the same standards as the YB-24 except that they were armed with .303-caliber machine guns as defensive armament. They were painted in a brown and green camouflage pattern with black undersides and were used as long range transports by the RAF. *(Piet collection)*

Six of the seven aircraft originally ordered as YB-24s were completed to early B-24D standards. B-24D, 40-697, was one of those six aircraft, and this photograph provides evidence that the six airframes in the YB-24 order that were completed as B-24Ds were not the same six aircraft that became LB-30As. *(National Archives)*

LB-30B LIBERATOR I

The gun pack with the four 20-mm cannon can be seen beneath the fuselage of this Liberator I. Also note the radar antenna under the outer wing panel. These aircraft had round engine nacelles without the side scoops found on most later Liberator variants. *(National Archives)*

Realizing that if they lost the Battle of the Atlantic, they would lose the war, Great Britain looked for ways to increase their effectiveness in combating German U-boats that were sinking merchant ships transporting materials across the North Atlantic. Short and medium ranged aircraft simply could not provide air cover above these vulnerable ships for their entire crossing. Twenty aircraft were taken from the original French order and delivered to the RAF's Coastal Command for use as long range anti-submarine patrol aircraft.

These twenty aircraft were designated LB-30Bs and named Liberator Is by the British. RAF serials AM910 through AM929 were assigned. They were fitted with a belly fairing containing four 20-mm cannon for use in strafing U-boats caught on the surface. Depth charges were carried inside the bomb bay.

Search radar antennas were added under the wings and on the aft fuselage where a series of long masts extended vertically and horizontally. The radar helped the Liberator I's crew locate submarines on the surface of the ocean beyond visual range and in weather conditions which restricted visibility.

A side view of a Liberator I shows the high antenna masts for the search radar on top of the aft fuselage. Similar masts extend horizontally from the sides of the fuselage, but they appear as black marks on the fuselage in this view. *(National Archives)*

B-24A

The RB-24As used by the U. S. Army Ferry Command were painted in the same brown and green camouflage used on British aircraft, but the vertical surfaces as well as the undersides were painted flat black. Large U. S. flags were painted on both sides of the nose and on top of the fuselage. **(Lloyd collection)**

An order for 120 B-24As was originally placed by the U. S. Army on behalf of the French government. They were to be armed with two .30-caliber machine guns in the tail and single .50-caliber weapons in the waist and nose positions. However, France was defeated by Germany before any of these aircraft could be delivered. The first twenty were delivered to the RAF as LB-30Bs,

and nine were used for testing by the USAAC as B-24As. These nine, serial numbers 40-2369 through 40-2377, were subsequently redesignated RB-24As to denote their restricted non-combat status, and they were turned over to the Army Ferry Command where they were used as long range transports. The remaining eighty-five aircraft from the original French order were completed as B-24Cs and B-24Ds.

The engines are started on a RB-24A prior to a flight. Note that the propellers are natural metal instead of the usual black found on later aircraft. The RB-24A also had the round engine cowlings without the scoops on the sides. **(National Archives)**

LIBERATOR II & LB-30

The Boulton-Paul turret with its four .303-caliber machine guns can be seen on this Liberator II. Note that it is located further aft that the Martin turrets used on American Liberators. **(Lloyd collection)**

The Liberator II was the first version to have the lengthened nose section which increased the overall length from 63 feet 9 inches to 66 feet 4 inches. This longer nose would remain standard on all subsequent variants of the Liberator. The Liberator II also had self-sealing fuel tanks and Curtiss Electric propellers which could be identified by their longer hubs. The British installed Boulton-Paul power operated turrets in the dorsal and tail positions, and each of these had four .303-cali-

ber machine guns. Manually operated .303-caliber guns were mounted in pairs in each of the waist positions.

A total of 140 were delivered to the RAF, but 75 were taken over by the U. S. Army on an emergency basis after the Japanese attack on Pearl Harbor. These aircraft, designated LB-30s by the Army, were used as both transports and bombers in the Pacific during America's early days in the war against Japan. They differed from the British Liberator IIs in that they had .50-caliber machine guns as defensive armament. A Martin powered turret with two guns was installed in the dorsal position, and a manually operated twin mount was used in the tail. Single machine guns were mounted in the waist windows and nose glazing. Twenty-three LB-30s were subsequently transferred to the RAF.

Liberator IIs had Curtiss Electric propellers instead of the Hamilton-Standard props used on other Liberators. These could be distinguished by their longer hubs. Also note the longer nose section that would remain standard on subsequent variants, and the details of the round engine nacelles, the cowl flaps, and the exhausts.

(Lloyd collection)

The U. S. Army data block on "Jungle Queen" indicates that this aircraft was one of seventy-five LB-30s taken over by the U. S. Army on an emergency basis shortly after the Japanese attack on Pearl Harbor. It retains the British serial number, AL640, although it is stenciled as AL-640 in the data block. Notice the blistered side window on the canopy. **(Lloyd collection)**

B-24C

Only nine B-24Cs were built, but they introduced the Martin top turret and the cowl rings with the cheek scoops on each side. Note that there is no navigator's astrodome on top of the lengthened nose and that the pitot probes are located low on the side of the nose section. **(National Archives)**

Only nine B-24Cs were delivered to the U. S. Army, and these were originally part of the French order. Like the Liberator II and LB-30, they had the lengthened nose section that brought overall length up to 66 feet 4 inches. They had the Martin power operated turret in the top of the fuselage, and a Consolidated A-6 turret was installed in the tail position for the first time. Single .50-caliber machine guns were mounted in the two waist positions and in the nose glazing. The final defensive weapon was a single machine gun mounted to fire down through an opening in the lower aft fuselage. These Liberators also had self-sealing fuel tanks and were generally considered to be combat ready, however they were redesignated RB-24Cs and used only for training purposes. Deliveries were completed in February 1942.

B-24Cs were powered by four Pratt & Whitney R-1830-41 engines, and for the first time, the two cheek scoops appeared on the cowl rings, thus giving the nacelles an oval cross section. These would remain a standard feature on all subsequent variants except the PB4Y-2 Privateer which had scoops mounted in the top and bottom of each cowl ring.

The B-24C was the first U. S. production version of the Liberator to feature power operated gun turrets. In addition to the Martin dorsal turret, a Consolidated A-6 turret was installed in the tail position. The original design for this turret had staggered guns as shown here.

(National Archives)

A close-up provides a good look at the cheek scoops on the sides of the cowl rings. Beginning with the B-24C, these scoops would remain standard on all future Liberator variants, however the PB4Y-2 Privateer would have a different arrangement with scoops on the top and bottom of each cowl ring. **(Lloyd collection)**

B-24D

The B-24D was the first version of the Liberator to be built in large numbers. "Moby Dick" was one of many Liberators to complete a hundred or more combat missions. It was assigned to the 320th Bomb Squadron of the 90th Bomb Group. *(Jones collection)*

Once America entered the war, production of all military aircraft was continually increased to levels beyond anything thought possible only a few months earlier. With a total of 2,696 being delivered, the B-24D became the first variant to be produced in large quantities and the first to be manufactured under the pool system by several plants. B-24Ds were built at San Diego, Fort Worth, and Tulsa. Except for a few of the seventy-five LB-30s taken over by the USAAC after the attack on Pearl Harbor, the B-24D was the first variant to be flown into combat by U. S. Army crews.

Some B-24Ds had R-1830-43 engines, but all B-24D-DTs (those built at Tulsa) were fitted with the R-1830-65. The change to this powerplant was made with the B-24D-140-CO production block at San Diego, and the B-24D-25-CF block at Fort Worth. The engines turned

The opposite side of "Moby Dick's" nose art is shown here along with a spotter plane named "Moby Dick JR." When cheek guns were added to the nose section, the pitot probes were moved to a higher location on the sides of the nose. *(Jones collection)*

Hamilton Standard propellers which were eleven feet seven inches in diameter.

Initially, the armament was the same as had been installed on the B-24C, but several changes were made to the nose and ventral armaments as production continued. To increase the firepower to the front, .50-caliber machine guns were added in the cheek positions on each side of the nose beginning with the B-24D-15-CO production block. Although these weapons helped to some extent, they were far from the ultimate solution to the Liberator's inadequate firepower to the front. The nose compartment was too cramped to use them effectively, visibility was limited, and their fields of fire would not allow them to be fired directly ahead of the aircraft. The addition of the cheek guns caused the two pitot probes to be moved upwards to a higher location on the sides of the nose, and they were also moved further aft. The forward nose gun was moved from its original position above the bomb sighting glass to a location below the glass. This further limited its field of fire, and in some cases, it was mounted in a fixed position and wired to be fired by the pilot.

Even with the two additional cheek guns, combat experience proved that the Liberator still lacked adequate defensive firepower to the front. Some engineers in the Fifth Air Force took a Consolidated A-6 turret that had been salvaged from the tail of a damaged Liberator, and they grafted it onto the nose of one of their B-24Ds. This was the first experiment involving the installation of a nose turret on a B-24D. It proved so successful that many more B-24Ds were modified at field depots where Consolidated A-6 turrets were mated to the nose. Eventually, a power operated nose turret became a production standard on later variants beginning with the twenty-sixth B-24G.

A single ventral .50-caliber machine gun had been mounted through a window or hatch in the lower aft fuselage of the B-24C. Known as the tunnel gun, it was also installed on early B-24Ds, and small scanning windows were added on each side of the lower aft fuselage. But this single weapon proved to be inadequate for protecting the aircraft from below.

The first solution to the problem was the addition of a remotely sighted Bendix turret, but gunners experienced motion sickness trying to acquire targets and fire the turret's guns while using the crude remote sight. As a result, only 287 B-24Ds were produced with this turret before the change was made back to the tunnel gun with B-24D-15-CO, 41-23970.

The final answer to protecting the aircraft from below was the installation of a retractable Sperry ball turret which was also used on late versions of the B-17 Flying Fortress. This turret was added beginning with B-24D-140-CO, 41-41164. It remained a production standard for all subsequent Liberator bomber variants except the B-24L and some B-24Ms. It also was not installed on the PB4Y-2 Privateer, C-87 Liberator Express, or C-109 tanker.

On occasion, the ball turret was removed, and a retractable radar dome was mounted in its place. These radars were used for different purposes including surface search, and this type of radar was often found on Navy PB4Y-1s which were originally taken from B-24D stocks. Another type of radar mounted in place of the ball turret was used for blind bombing through overcast conditions, and Liberators equipped with these radars were known as pathfinders.

To increase range, auxiliary fuel tanks were added in the outer wing panels beginning with the B-24D-10-CF block, and at the same time provisions were included to carry fuel tanks in the bomb bay. Some B-24Ds that operated in Alaska were fitted with YAGI radar antennas under the wings.

B-24Ds in the Royal Air Force were known as Liberator IIIs. They had the additional fuel tanks and most were used for patrol duties with the Coastal Command. The Martin dorsal turret of the B-24D was replaced with a Boulton-Paul turret with four .303-caliber machine guns. In addition to the armament changes, Liberator IIIs had an ASV surface search radar. They were also the first RAF variant to be armed with rockets carried on small wings on each side of the lower fuselage. Others had searchlights under the wings to search for submarines at night. Liberator IIIAs were identical to standard USAAF B-24Ds, and they were transferred to the RAF Coastal Command in 1942.

"Playmate" was an all black B-24D-20-CF, serial number 42-63980, and it was used for clandestine operations in the form of night leaflet drops. Throughout the war, many Liberators were used for special operations, and in some cases they were extensively modified to perform these missions. *(Lloyd collection)*

A top view of a B-24D provides a good look at the Liberator's planform. *(National Archives)*

Above and right: Even with the additional cheek guns mounted on each side of the nose, the defensive firepower to the front of the aircraft proved to be very inadequate. Some B-24Ds had Consolidated turrets grafted onto the nose. To provide sufficient room for the bombardier beneath the turret, those modified at the Oklahoma City Modification Center had an enlarged lower nose section, and as a result, they were called "droop snoots." Again note the staggered gun arrangement of the original Consolidated turret design.

(Both, Lloyd collection)

B-24D

DROOP SNOOT NOSE AND TURRET ADDED TO SOME B-24Ds AND PB4Y-1s AT FIELD MODIFICATION CENTERS

NOSE GEAR DOORS OPENED INWARD

DETAIL & SCALE © COPYRIGHT DRAWING BY LLOYD S. JONES

B-24D DETAILS

NOSE COMPARTMENT INTERIOR DETAILS

Above left: The bombardier's seat can be seen in this view that looks forward inside the nose compartment. This photograph suggests how cramped it really was inside the Liberator's nose.   (National Archives)

Above right: A compass was the major item on the right side of the nose compartment. Note the snap-in covering on the side of the fuselage.   (National Archives)

The left side was far more cluttered than the right. The bombardier's quadrant contains the manual bomb release handles, and the control panel that selects which bombs are to be dropped is low on the side of the fuselage. The intervalometer is next to the quadrant on the framework for the glazing.   (National Archives)

This view looks down into the nose compartment and shows the location of the forward gun mounted low in the framework for the glazing. The two cheek guns with their ammunition belts are also visible, but the restricted movement of the guns inside the cramped compartment is obvious.   (National Archives)

COCKPIT DETAILS

An overall view of the B-24D's cockpit reveals the D-shaped control yokes. Although some Liberators had the yokes with an open top as shown on page 40, most had ones like those shown here. The magnetic compass is the prominent feature at the center of the cockpit. The basic layout of the cockpit remained the same for all Liberator variants, and what changes were made were relatively minor. They were usually related to improved equipment like the autopilot or electronic gear.
(National Archives)

At the forward end of the overhead panel was the compass receiver control box, and to the rear of it was the command receiver control box. A placard can be seen further aft on the overhead. Curtains could be opened outward to reduce the sun's heat inside the cockpit.
(National Archives)

Instruments immediately in front of the pilot included the free air temperature gauge, the suction gauge, flap indicator, air speed indicator, turn indicator, and the turn and bank indicator. *(National Archives)*

Engine instruments were located on the co-pilot's side, and these included manifold pressure gauges, tachometers, engine cylinder temperature gauges, and oil temperature gauges. *(National Archives)*

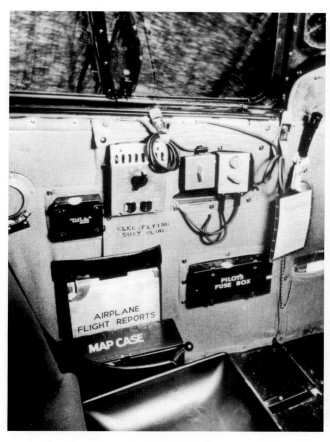

The two smaller silver boxes on the left side of the cockpit were the pilot's intercom controls. Also located on this side were the case for the airplane's flight reports, the map case, and the pilot's fuse box. The larger silver box was where the pilot plugged in his electrical flying suit and controlled the warmth it provided at high altitudes. *(National Archives)*

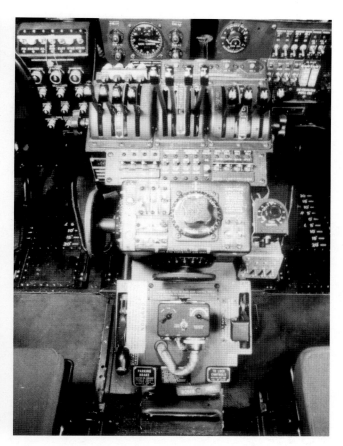

The center stand had the propeller, supercharger, and engine controls as well as the trim wheels. Numerous switches were also located on the center pedestal, and among these were switches for the propellers, intercoolers, and the cockpit heaters. The radio compass is on the instrument panel just above the stand, as is the anti-icing rheostat. *(National Archives)*

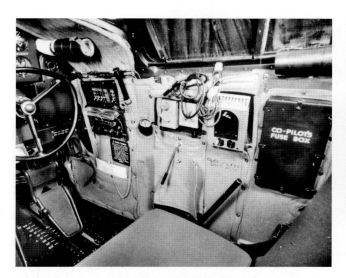

The co-pilot's intercom controls took up much of the space on the right side of the cockpit. The co-pilot's fuse box was near the back of the seat, and the panel for his electrically heated flying suit is also visible. *(National Archives)*

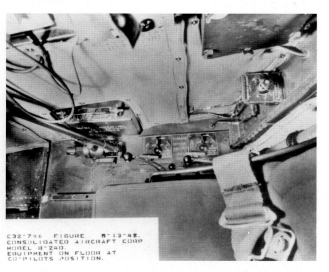

Emergency fire extinguisher pull handles were mounted on the floor of the cockpit between the co-pilot's seat and the right side wall. They were just aft of the emergency hydraulic hand pump. Forward is to the left in this view. *(National Archives)*

FUSELAGE INTERIOR DETAILS

This photograph looks up into the Martin top turret. The aft ends of the machine guns are visible up inside the dome. Two yellow bottles provided oxygen for the gunner. (National Archives)

The Liberator had a considerable amount of radio equipment. This is the liaison receiver on the radio operator's table. Note the transmitter key to the right of the receiver. (National Archives)

The liaison antenna tuning unit was located aft of the radio operator's table on some aircraft, but its position varied within the forward fuselage compartment. (National Archives)

A large liaison transmitter set was mounted under the radio operator's table. This view looks forward and to the right in the forward fuselage compartment. (National Archives)

Additional liaison tuning units were stowed near the radio operator's station. The tuning unit was part of the transmitter equipment seen under the radio operator's table in the middle right photograph. (National Archives)

Command radio equipment was located in the over-wing center section. From left to right, these include three command receivers, two command transmitters, and a large compass receiver. (National Archives)

C32-837 FIGURE 11-3-42
CONSOLIDATED AIRCRAFT CORP
MODEL 824-D.
BOOSTER PUMP AND HOSE
CONNECTIONS TO AUXILIARY
BOMB BAY-FULL CELLS.

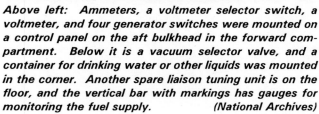

Above left: Ammeters, a voltmeter selector switch, a voltmeter, and four generator switches were mounted on a control panel on the aft bulkhead in the forward compartment. Below it is a vacuum selector valve, and a container for drinking water or other liquids was mounted in the corner. Another spare liaison tuning unit is on the floor, and the vertical bar with markings has gauges for monitoring the fuel supply. (National Archives)

Above right: Long range fuel tanks could be carried in the bomb bays, and these large bladders can be seen strapped into place in this view that looks aft into the forward bomb bay. Hoses, connectors, and a booster pump for the fuel are also visible. (National Archives)

C32-839 FIGURE 11-3-42
CONSOLIDATED AIRCRAFT CORP
MODEL 824-D.
VIEW LOOKING FORWARD
FROM STA. 7.0.

Both waist guns can be seen in this photograph that looks toward the rear of the aircraft in the aft fuselage compartment. Also note the opening and the mount for the tunnel gun, however the gun itself is not installed in this case. (National Archives)

This view looks forward in the aft fuselage compartment toward the wing center section. Again, the two waist guns can be seen in their stowed position. Oxygen bottles are located on the right side of the aircraft and in the background. (National Archives)

DEFENSIVE ARMAMENT DETAILS

Above left: In the original configuration for the B-24D's nose armament, a single .50-caliber machine gun was mounted through a ball socket above the bomb aiming window. Later, the two cheek guns were added to increase defensive firepower to the front, but neither of these weapons could be fired directly ahead of the aircraft, and they proved to be inadequate in combat.
(USAFM)

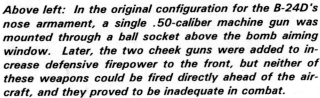

Above right: Because it interfered with the bombardier when he was sighting through the bomb sight, the forward gun was subsequently relocated to a position beneath the bomb aiming window. The two cheek guns remained in a similar arrangement to their earlier configuration, but note the small window added just aft of the gun's mounting socket on the left side. (Lloyd collection)

Right: A view inside the nose compartment shows the lower gun and the right cheek gun as well as their ammunition feed belts. The bombardier had to assume a prone position to fire the lower gun, and in some cases it was mounted in a fixed position and wired so that it could be fired by the pilot.
(Lloyd collection)

The original Martin top turret with the lower dome design is illustrated on top of this B-24D. Two oval shaped hatches were located just aft of the turret, and they contained inflatable life rafts. The left one is shown here in the open position. Also note the open hatch located between the turret and the top of the canopy.
(Lloyd collection)

On the B-24D, the waist windows were not enclosed like they were on some later versions, however they could be closed by panels when not being used. A single .50-caliber machine gun in each window remained the standard waist armament for all Liberator variants, although some had twin-gun mounts installed by units in the field.
(Lloyd collection)

To provide defensive fire below the aircraft, Liberators initially had a single .50-caliber machine gun mounted through an opening in the lower fuselage. It was installed in B-24Cs and early B-24Ds. (Lloyd collection)

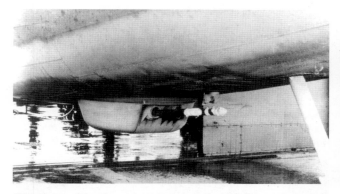

Starting with the seventy-seventh B-24D, a remotely controlled belly turret was installed. However, it was also ineffective, and gunners became nauseous trying to aim and fire it through the remote sight. As a result, it was only installed on 287 B-24Ds, then the change was made back to the tunnel gun. (Lloyd collection)

A gunner mans the tunnel gun in a B-24D. The gun was ineffective and very awkward to aim and fire.
(Lloyd collection)

Beginning with B-24D-140-CO, 41-41164, the belly armament was changed once again to a retractable Sperry ball turret. This remained the standard lower armament on most subsequent Liberator bomber variants except for the B-24L and some B-24Ms. On occasion, these turrets were replaced with retractable radar domes used for surface search or blind bombing. The ball turret also was not used on the PB4Y-2 Privateer. (Lloyd collection)

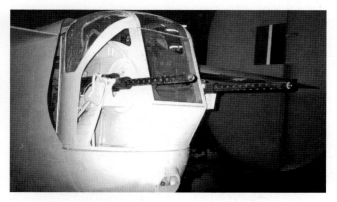

The B-24C was the first version of the Liberator to be fitted with an A-6 turret in the tail position, and this remained standard on the B-24D and most subsequent variants except for the B-24L. Built by Consolidated, the turret was often called the Consair turret, and it was also used in the nose position on many Liberators, particularly B-24Js. A lightweight version, known as the A-6B would subsequently be developed. (Lloyd collection)

LANDING GEAR DETAILS

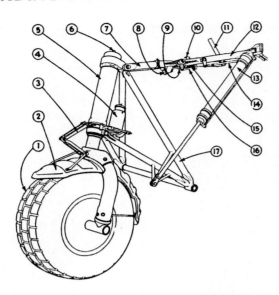

1. Tire
2. Mudguard
3. Oleo Scissor
4. Shimmy Damper
5. Oleo Strut
6. Filler Fitting
7. Forward Drag Link
8. Latch Switch
9. Drag Link Latch
10. Drag Link Booster Spring
11. Drag Link Booster Spring
12. Aft Drag Link
13. Hydraulic Cylinder
14. Latch Link
15. Latch Linkage Spring
16. Latch Link
17. V Strut

Details of the nose gear are identified in this drawing taken from the Liberator's Erection and Maintenance Manual. (USAFM)

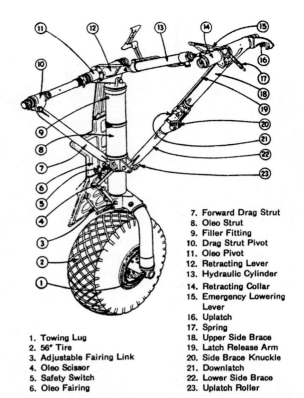

1. Towing Lug
2. 56" Tire
3. Adjustable Fairing Link
4. Oleo Scissor
5. Safety Switch
6. Oleo Fairing
7. Forward Drag Strut
8. Oleo Strut
9. Filler Fitting
10. Drag Strut Pivot
11. Oleo Pivot
12. Retracting Lever
13. Hydraulic Cylinder
14. Retracting Collar
15. Emergency Lowering Lever
16. Uplatch
17. Spring
18. Upper Side Brace
19. Latch Release Arm
20. Side Brace Knuckle
21. Downlatch
22. Lower Side Brace
23. Uplatch Roller

This drawing identifies the features on the Liberator's main landing gear. This is the left main gear, and the right gear was simply a mirror image. (USAFM)

The nose gear strut was a single fork design with the fork being on the left side of the wheel.

Details of the spokes on the right side of the nose gear are shown here, however both sides of the wheel were often protected by covers to prevent mud and other debris from getting into the spokes.

Taken from within the nose compartment, this unusual photograph shows details of the nose gear from the front. Note the mudguard that prevented mud from being splattered up inside the well. (National Archives)

Above left: The high wing of the Liberator required a very strong landing gear with a long strut. The main strut was reinforced with a forward drag strut and a side brace. This is the left main landing gear.

Above right: Details inside the left gear well are visible here. The main circular part of the well remained uncovered by doors even when the gear was retracted. A retractable landing light was located just forward of the gear well under each wing.

Hydraulic lines ran down the strut to the brakes inside the wheel. This is the outboard side of the left main wheel and tire.

Details on the inside of the wheel are shown in this close-up. The main strut had doors attached to its inboard side that covered it when the gear was retracted.

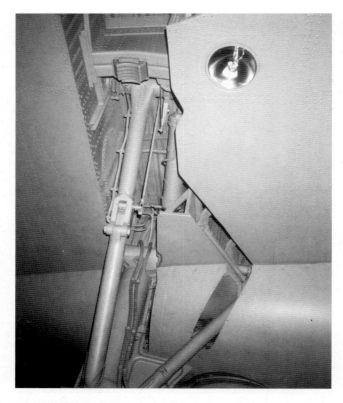

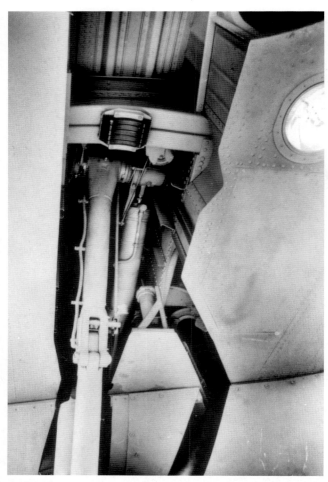

Above left: The inner part of the right main gear well is illustrated in this view that looks up and inboard. Notice how part of the well actually extended into the nacelle of the inboard engine.

Above right: The small hydraulic cylinder that actuated the right main gear is visible from this angle.

(National Archives)

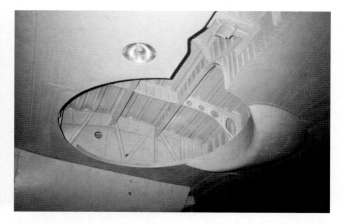

Hydraulic lines ran down the entire length of the main strut and entered the wheel through the hollow axle. The strut, doors, and wheel were usually painted the same color as the underside of the wings.

An aerodynamic fairing smoothed the airflow behind the wheel and tire when the gear was retracted. Details inside the outer section of the right main gear well are illustrated here.

POWERPLANT DETAILS

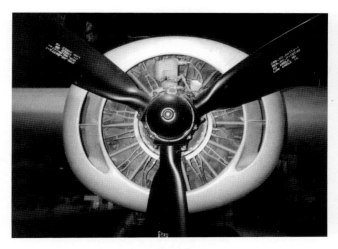

A front view shows the cylinders, rods, and wiring on one of the R-1830-43 powerplants.

When the cowl flaps were closed, the engine nacelle was very streamlined and slender.

With the panels removed or opened, details on the inboard side of the left outboard (Number 1) engine are revealed.   (National Archives)

This is the outboard side of the same Number 1 engine shown at left. In both views, note how the exhaust is routed to the turbosupercharger.   (National Archives)

Mechanics labor on the engines of a Liberator in the field. Much work could be done without having to remove the engines from the aircraft.   (Lloyd collection)

Wastegates for the turbosuperchargers were under each engine nacelle. Turbosuperchargers increased the aircraft's performance at higher altitudes. (Lloyd collection)

FUSELAGE DETAILS

Above: Early B-24Ds, like B-24D-CO, 41-11935, had the pitot probes mounted well forward and about midway up on the sides of the nose. They also did not have the cheek guns installed. Note the small window on the side of the fuselage adjacent to the radio operator's station. This window was standard on the B-24D and all subsequent Liberator variants.   (Lloyd collection)

Left: After the cheek guns were added, the pitot probes were moved to a higher position on the nose, and they were also moved further aft behind the scanning window. This was done to help prevent gun gasses from entering the small hole at the end of the probe. Even after power operated turrets became the standard nose armament, the two pitot probes remained in this position.

The left pitot probe and the standard window arrangement for the forward fuselage on a B-24D with cheek guns are shown here. Again notice the small window on the side of the fuselage for the forward compartment. Most B-24Ds had flat sliding windows on each side of the cockpit.   (Lloyd collection)

Photographs indicate that some B-24Ds had blistered sliding windows on the sides of the cockpit, and this was true for subsequent variants as well. The blistered windows were of particular value on patrol missions when the Liberator's crew was searching for shipping, submarines, or even features or objects on the ground.

WING DETAILS

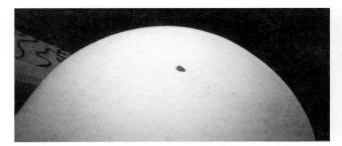

Early versions of the Liberator had small, teardrop-shaped, navigation lights on the top and bottom of each wing tip. This is the red light beneath the left wing tip.

The green light under the right wing tip is shown here from behind. A similar light was located in the corresponding position on top of the wing tip.

Center, left and right: Most later variants of the Liberator had a single light on the edge of the wing tip instead of the double light arrangement. This new design was first used during the B-24H production run, but many B-24Js had the earlier light configuration as seen in the top two photos. B-24Ls, B-24Ms, and PB4Y-2 Privateers all had this later configuration.

The ailerons were made of a metal framework that was covered with fabric, and each had a trim tab near the inboard end. Also note the four hinges that attach the aileron to the wing.

Details of the extended left flap are illustrated in this view. Notice how part of the aerodynamic fairing behind the gear well extends below the flap well.

(National Archives)

TAIL DETAILS

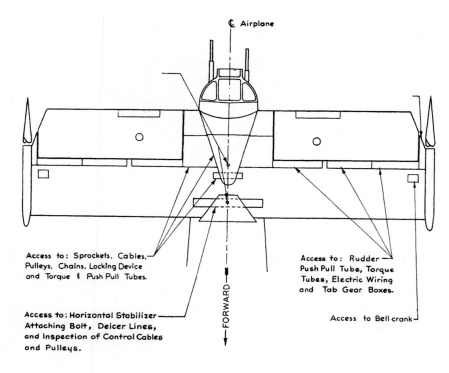

℄ Airplane

Access to: Sprockets, Cables, Pulleys, Chains, Locking Device and Torque & Push Pull Tubes.

Access to: Horizontal Stabilizer Attaching Bolt, Deicer Lines, and Inspection of Control Cables and Pulleys.

FORWARD

Access to: Rudder Push Pull Tube, Torque Tubes, Electric Wiring and Tab Gear Boxes.

Access to Bell crank

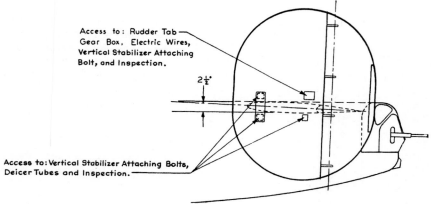

Access to: Rudder Tab Gear Box, Electric Wires, Vertical Stabilizer Attaching Bolt, and Inspection.

$2\frac{1}{2}°$

Access to: Vertical Stabilizer Attaching Bolts, Deicer Tubes and Inspection.

An overall view of the Liberator's empennage shows that there was no dihedral on the horizontal tail, and the vertical tails were mounted at a ninety-degree angle to the horizontal tail. Also notice the bumper skid under the aft fuselage. It rests on a small stool to help support the rear of the aircraft. *(National Archives)*

The vertical tails were oval shaped and symmetrical, and a small trim tab was located on the trailing edge of each rudder. The rudders and elevators were covered with fabric. This particular Liberator is one of the USAAF B-24Ds transferred to the Navy as an early PB4Y-1. *(National Archives)*

DIMENSION DRAWINGS

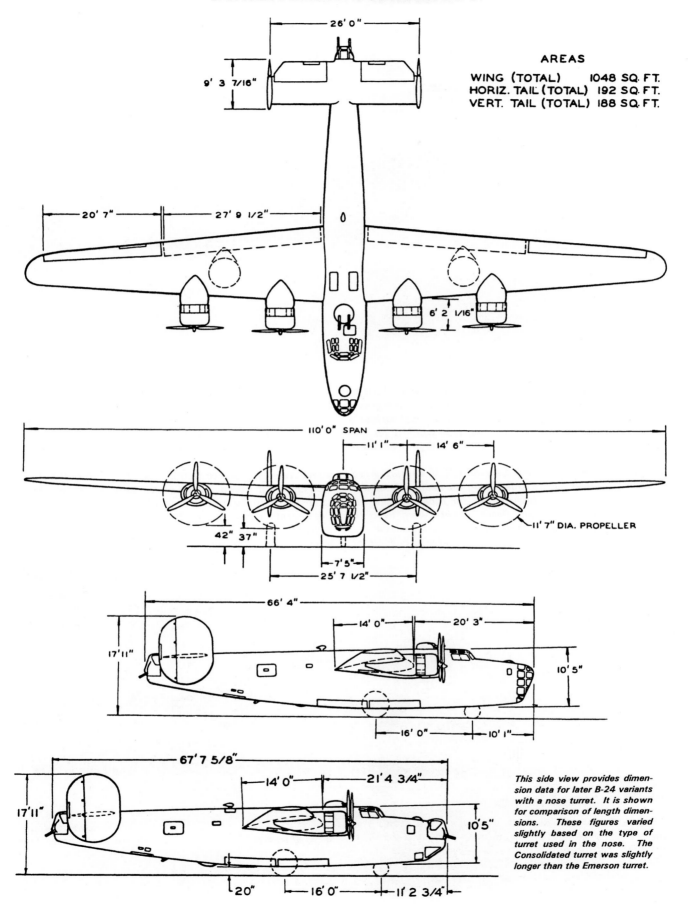

AREAS

WING (TOTAL) 1048 SQ. FT.
HORIZ. TAIL (TOTAL) 192 SQ. FT.
VERT. TAIL (TOTAL) 188 SQ. FT.

26' 0"

9' 3 7/16"

20' 7"   27' 9 1/2"

6' 2 1/16"

110' 0" SPAN

11' 1"   14' 6"

11' 7" DIA. PROPELLER

42" 37"

7' 5"

25' 7 1/2"

66' 4"

14' 0"   20' 3"

17' 11"

10' 5"

16' 0"   10' 1"

67' 7 5/8"

14' 0"   21' 4 3/4"

17' 11"

10' 5"

20"   16' 0"   11' 2 3/4"

This side view provides dimension data for later B-24 variants with a nose turret. It is shown for comparison of length dimensions. These figures varied slightly based on the type of turret used in the nose. The Consolidated turret was slightly longer than the Emerson turret.

LIBERATOR GR V

Above: The fairing under the chin of the Liberator GR V was for the ASV radar. This aircraft is painted in a green and gray camouflage scheme with white vertical surfaces and undersides. Note the blistered side window on the cockpit.
(Lloyd collection)

Below: Liberator III and Liberator GR V aircraft were sometimes fitted with a small wing on each side of the lower fuselage. Four launch rails for rockets were attached to each wing, and these rockets were used to attack shipping or submarines caught on the surface.
(Lloyd collection)

Like the Liberator III and IIIA, the Liberator GR V was based on the B-24D airframe, however it was equipped with an improved radar designed specifically to look for ships. With this new radar, the Liberator GR Vs were utilized exclusively for patrol missions, and they were assigned to the RAF's Coastal Command. Additionally, some were provided to Number 10 Squadron of the Royal Canadian Air Force. The Air-to-Surface Vessel (ASV) radar was usually mounted in a fairing under the chin of the aircraft, however reports indicate that in some cases it was located in a retractable cylindrical dome mounted in place of the ball turret.

COLOR GALLERY

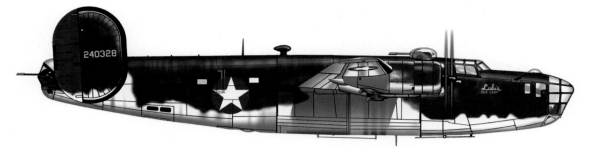

"Lulu´s OLE LADY" was a B-24D used for coastal patrol duties. It is painted in the Olive Drab over white paint scheme commonly applied to USAAF aircraft used for this mission.

"Prince Charming" was formerly named *"Snow White."* This B-24D Desert Pink over Neutral Gray B-24D was lost during one of the raids against the oil fields at Ploesti, Rumania.

The standard Olive Drab over Neutral Gray paint scheme was applied to this B-24J assigned to the 465th Bomb Group in Italy.

The red tail markings on this B-24M indicate that it was assigned to the 461st Bomb Group which was part of the 15th Air Force in Italy,

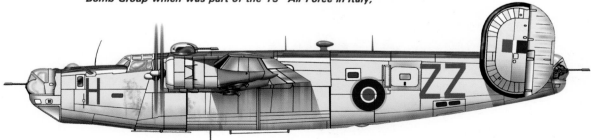

This Liberator VI was flown by Number 220 Squadron of the Royal Air Forces' Coastal Command.

LIBERATOR COLORS

Some B-24As operated by the Ferry Command had the British Dark Earth and Dark Green camouflage on the upper surfaces. Black was applied to vertical surfaces and the undersides. *(Piet collection)*

Above: Most B-24As were delivered to the USAAC in the Olive Drab over Neutral Gray paint scheme. The national insignia with the red disc at the center was applied to both fuselage sides as well as the top of the left wing and bottom of the right. U.S. ARMY was lettered in black beneath the wings. *(Piet collection)*

Below: This B-24D was painted in the Olive Drab over white scheme used on Army aircraft that performed maritime patrol duties. *(Meyer via Piet)*

Above: Many Liberators that operated in the desert areas of Africa were painted in a tan color called Desert Pink. FS 31575 is a close match.
(via Ethell and Piet)

Right: These B-24Ds are painted in the standard Olive Drab over Neutral Gray scheme used in most areas of operation. (Piet collection)

Below: Liberators used for training in the United States usually had large numbers painted on the forward fuselage, and these were often repeated on the vertical tail. Note the national insignia with the rectangles added to the sides and the red surround used for a short time in 1943.
(Piet collection)

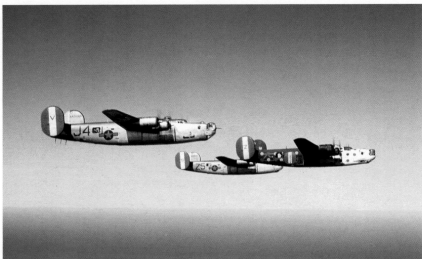

Above: "TUBARAO" was a B-24J assigned to the 491st Bomb Group. This war weary Liberator was painted with colorful yellow and green stripes and used as a marshaling aircraft. Bombers would form on these aircraft as they assembled for raids.
(Austrella via Piet)

Left: B-24Js of the 458th Bomb Group form on the marshaling aircraft for that unit. A white forward fuselage and polka dots of various colors were the high visibility markings for this Liberator. (Piet collection)

Below: This B-24H flew missions with the Fifth Photo Group.
(Astrella via Piet)

LIBERATOR NOSE ART

"Home Breaker" was a B-24H assigned to the 706th Bomb Squadron. (Krassman via Ethell and Piet)

Another B-24H used by the 706th BS was named "Dinky Duck." (Krassman via Ethell and Piet)

"Lazy Lou" was also an Olive Drab and Neutral Gray Liberator assigned to the 706th Bomb Squadron. (Krassman via Ethell and Piet)

"Naughty Nan" was assigned to the 705th BS. Forty-one mission markings are painted just below the windscreen. (Krassman via Ethell and Piet)

"OLD FAITHFUL" had nose art on the right side of the nose, and this was common practice on many Liberators. This is another 706th BS aircraft. (Krassman via Ethell and Piet)

B-24J-CO-150, 44-40208, was named "KENTUCKY BELLE." Three red boxcars and a parachute bomb are painted next to the numerous mission markings. (Krassman via Ethell and Piet)

The best known nose art used on any Liberator was "THE DRAGON AND HIS TAIL." It was applied to a B-24J of the 43rd Bomb Group. (via Ethell and Piet)

A famous B-17G was named "Shoo Shoo Baby," but the name was also applied to B-24H, 42-95157, of the 704th Bomb Squadron. (Krassman via Ethell and Piet)

BRITISH LIBERATORS

Above: Early British Liberators, like this LB-30A, were painted in a Dark Green and Dark Earth camouflage pattern with black undersides.
(Piet collection)

Right: Later, the RAF took delivery of Liberators that were painted in the USAAF's Olive Drab over Neutral Gray scheme. (via Bamberger and Piet)

Below: This Liberator GR V is painted in a blue-gray and white camouflage scheme used for maritime patrol operations. It was operated by the Royal Canadian Air Force. (Meyer via Piet)

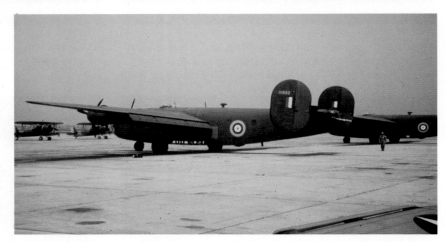

B-24D DETAILS IN COLOR
NOSE COMPARTMENT & ARMAMENT

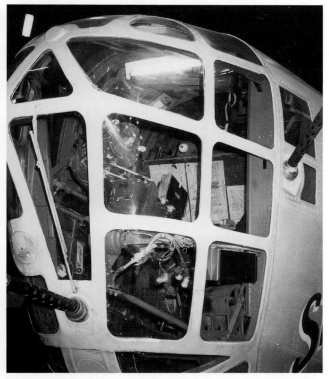

Above left and right: The design of the framing for the nose glazing as used on the B-24D and PB4Y-1 is revealed in these two views. Note that the right cheek gun is mounted through a ball socket in one of the clear panes of the nose glazing. The interior of the nose appears to be Interior Green, but evidence indicates that the forward crew compartments were usually Bronze Green or Dull Dark Green.

Below left: A wiper blade kept the bomb aiming window clear of rain or mud that splattered on it while the aircraft was taxiing. The mounting for the forward fixed machine gun is visible below the bomb aiming window.

Below right: The left cheek gun was located further aft than the right gun. It mounted through its own sighting window rather than through the nose glazing, and visibility for aiming this weapon was very limited. Also note the pitot probe and the navigator's astrodome on top of the nose section.

COCKPIT DETAILS

The cockpit in the Air Force Museum's B-24D remains virtually as it appeared when the aircraft was operational. Details of the pilot's instrument panel are shown here.

Features on the co-pilot's side of the instrument panel are illustrated in this view. The engine instruments were the co-pilot's primary responsibility.

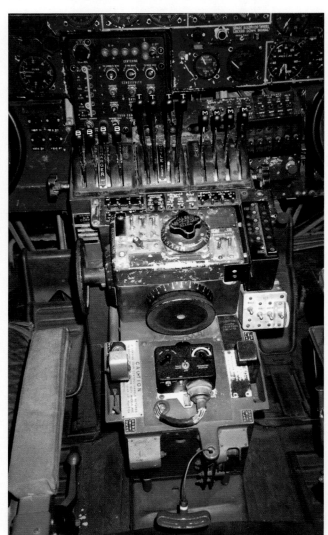

Supercharger controls, throttles, and propeller controls were located on the stand between the two seats. Trim control wheels are also visible.

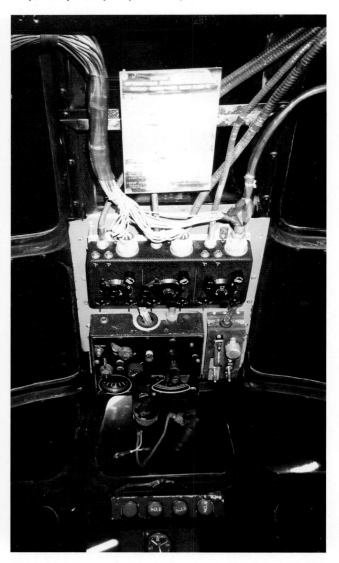

The overhead panel included the command receiver control box and the compass receiver control box.

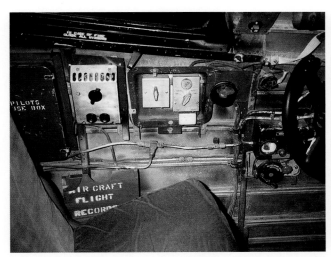

The large silver panel is where the pilot plugged in his electrically heated flying suit and controlled it's warmth. The two smaller silver panels were interphone controls.

Additional interphone controls and filter boxes were on the co-pilot's side. The panel for the co-pilot's electrically heated flight suit is also visible.

A plywood panel was located just aft of the pilot's seat, and a portable bottle of breathing oxygen was mounted between the seat and the panel.

There was no panel behind the co-pilot's seat, so details of the seat are visible in this photo. The radio operator's position was directly behind the co-pilot.

FORWARD COMPARTMENT DETAILS

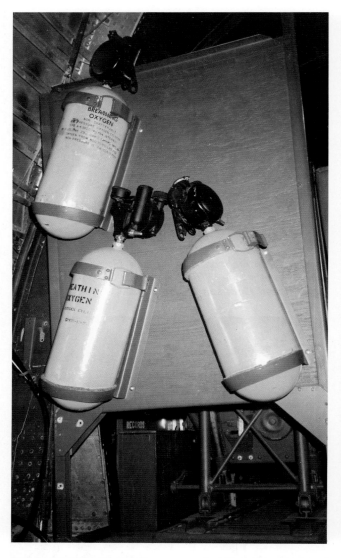

Three additional portable oxygen bottles were mounted on the aft side of the wooden panel behind the pilot's seat.

More oxygen bottles were located on the left side of the fuselage in the radio operator's compartment which was just aft of the cockpit.

Details of the radio operator's station are shown here. Except for the cockpit and nose compartment, the interior of the fuselage was sometimes left unpainted.

A liaison radio set was located under the radio operator's table. Additional liaison radios were stored in other locations near the radio operator's station.

BOMB BAY DETAILS

This view looks forward through the bomb bays. The slanted racks for the bombs are visible, as are the interior surfaces of the corrugated bomb bay doors.

Numerous wires and hydraulic plumbing lines were routed along the sides of the fuselage. This is the left side of the forward bomb bay looking aft.

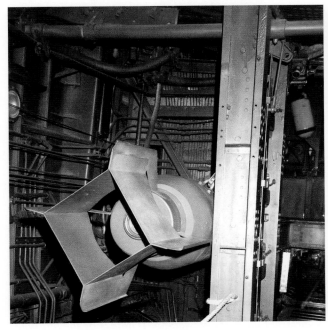

The left side of the forward bomb bay is shown again in this view looking forward from the aft bay. The interior surfaces of the bomb bays were painted Interior Green.

This view, and the one to the left, both show how bombs were attached to the vertical racks inside the bays.

AFT FUSELAGE COMPARTMENT

The B-24D had waist windows that had to be opened when the guns were fired. The panels that usually covered the windows were moved up to a location in the top of the fuselage above the windows. This is the waist window on the right side of the fuselage.

A retractable wind deflector was located just forward of each waist window. It was deployed as shown here when the window was open so that the guns could be fired. The deflectors retracted flush to the fuselage to reduce drag when the windows were closed.

Details of the right waist gun mount are visible here. The flexible belt that fed ammunition to the weapon hangs down from the storage box, and it is not connected to the gun in this photograph.

A different view shows additional details of the left waist gun and its mount. Note the cover for the window above the opening. Portable and fixed oxygen bottles are visible in the background.

Numerous oxygen bottles are visible in this view that was taken from a location even with the two waist windows. It looks forward in the aft fuselage compartment toward the bomb bays.

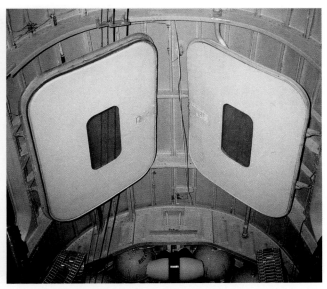

The two panels that covered the waist windows are shown here in their overhead stowed position. The interior of the aft compartment in this Liberator is painted with Chromate Yellow Primer, but it was left unpainted in many later B-24 variants.

A relief tube for the crew members in the aft fuselage compartment was mounted on the left side of the fuselage just aft of the waist gun position.

The entry to the rear gun turret is visible in the background of this photograph that looks aft from the waist gun positions.

PB4Y COLORS

Above: Although some early PB4Y-1s were delivered in the standard USAAF Olive Drab over Neutral Gray scheme and the Olive Drab over white camouflage, most were painted in this blue-gray and white scheme.

(Piet collection)

Left: This Non-Specular Sea Blue, Intermediate Blue, and white paint scheme was applied to most wartime PB4Y-2s. The Intermediate Blue was applied to the vertical surfaces of the aircraft. Fading of the darker color and spot touch-ups resulted in an uneven worn appearance, and it is difficult to distinguish between the Non-Specular Sea Blue and the Intermediate Blue colors. (via Ethell and Piet)

Like their USAAF counterparts, PB4Y-1s and PB4Y-2s sometimes were adorned with nose art and names as evidenced by "LOTTA TAYLE" painted on the right side of this Privateer. (Piet collection)

This PB4Y-2 displays victory flags in addition to its nose art and name "PEACE FEELER." Unfortunately, nose art like this would not be permitted in today's "politically correct" environment. (Piet collection)

In the postwar years, PB4Y-1s and PB4Y-2s were used for a variety of roles and were painted in unusual colors. This overall red Privateer was a drone controller at Point Magu. (U. S. Navy photograph via Piet)

This overall yellow PB4Y-1 was used for missile tests at Johnsville, Pennsylvania. At first glance, the missile may appear to be a Loon, which was the Navy's equivalent to the German V-1 buzz bomb, but it is actually a drone of a similar design. (Piet collection)

Anti-shipping missiles like this KDN-1 were also evaluated on the yellow PB4Y-1s at Johnsville. Note the antenna mounted low on the side of the forward fuselage. A color profile of this PB4Y-1 can be found on the next page. (Piet collection)

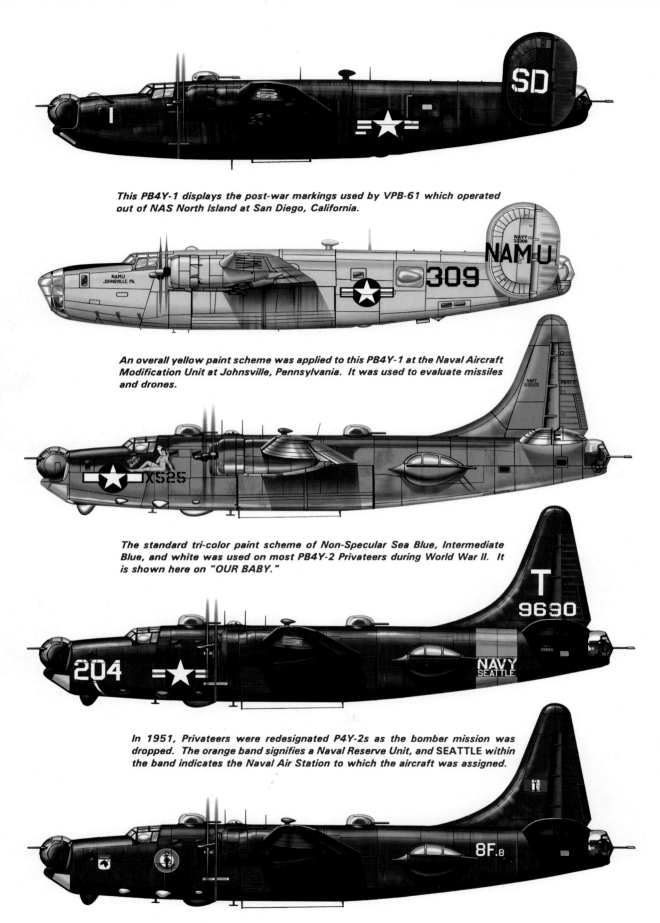

This PB4Y-1 displays the post-war markings used by VPB-61 which operated out of NAS North Island at San Diego, California.

An overall yellow paint scheme was applied to this PB4Y-1 at the Naval Aircraft Modification Unit at Johnsville, Pennsylvania. It was used to evaluate missiles and drones.

The standard tri-color paint scheme of Non-Specular Sea Blue, Intermediate Blue, and white was used on most PB4Y-2 Privateers during World War II. It is shown here on "OUR BABY."

In 1951, Privateers were redesignated P4Y-2s as the bomber mission was dropped. The orange band signifies a Naval Reserve Unit, and SEATTLE within the band indicates the Naval Air Station to which the aircraft was assigned.

This PB4Y-2 was operated by Escadrille 8F of the French Aeronavale.

XB-41

Above: One B-24D was converted to a heavily armed bomber escort and redesignated the XB-41. It was armed with fourteen .50-caliber machine guns, ten of which were mounted in turrets. But the extra weight of these weapons and their ammunition made the aircraft so heavy it was too slow to keep up with standard B-24s after they dropped their bomb load. It also suffered from stability problems. These problems, along with the ever increasing availability of long range fighter escorts, resulted in the cancellation of the XB-41 and the similar YB-40, several of which were converted from B-17 airframes. (Jones collection)

Center right: The XB-41 had a chin turret similar to the one used on B-17G Flying Fortresses. (Jones collection)

There were two dorsal turrets mounted on top of the XB-41. In this view, the turret in the left waist position is not installed. (Jones collection)

The left side waist position had a turret with two .50-caliber machine guns. The right waist position was a standard B-24D installation. (Jones collection)

B-24E

Except for slightly different propellers, the B-24E was externally identical to the B-24D. Therefore, it was very difficult to tell a B-24E from a B-24D if the serial number was not known. This is B-24E-25-FO, 42-7341.

(Lloyd collection)

The B-24E was very similar to the B-24D except that it had propellers with a slightly different blade design. A total of 801 were built at Willow Run, Tulsa, and Fort Worth, and those provided to the Royal Air Force were named Liberator IVs. USAAF B-24Es were retained in the United States for training purposes.

This B-24E was fitted with remotely controlled turrets and used to train B-29 gunners how to control and fire the guns through the use of remote scanners and sights. Note the sight mounted inside the blister that has been installed in the waist window. It appears that this B-24E-15-FO has been retrofitted with nose gear doors that opened externally, although this feature was not standard on B-24Es.

(Lloyd collection)

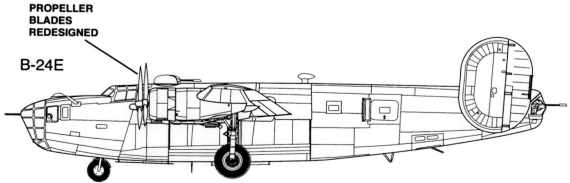

PROPELLER BLADES REDESIGNED

B-24E

DETAIL & SCALE © COPYRIGHT DRAWING BY LLOYD S. JONES

B-24G

After the first twenty-five B-24Gs were built with the same framed nose glazing as the B-24D and B-24E, the remaining B-24Gs were completed with an Emerson turret in the nose, making them the first production Liberators to be delivered from the factory with a nose turret. The B-24G was also the first version to have the nose gear doors that opened externally as a production standard. Note the deicing boots on the leading edges of the wings and tail surfaces of this B-24G-15-NT. (USAFM)

Combat experience with the B-24D had demonstrated inadequate defensive firepower to the front. Even after two cheek guns had been added, the Liberator was still quite vulnerable to head-on attacks by enemy fighters, due in part to the fact that the cheek guns could not be aimed directly ahead of the bomber. This problem was further complicated by poor visibility and inadequate fields of fire by these weapons. This left only one nose gun and the top turret to defend the aircraft from the front, and the top turret gunner had defensive responsibilities to the sides and above the bomber as well. As a result, some B-24Ds had Consolidated turrets, like those used in the tail, grafted onto their nose sections as a field fix for this deficiency. The improvement in defensive firepower to the front was instantly recognized, and nose turrets were ordered as a production standard beginning with the B-24G. Although the first twenty-five B-24Gs had the same front glazing as the B-24D and B-24E, an Emerson turret in the nose became standard on the twenty-sixth B-24G. All 430 B-24Gs were built by North American at their Dallas facility. Those provided to the RAF were known as Liberator Vs.

A Sperry A-5 automatic pilot was standard in all B-24Gs. Early B-24Gs had the same R-1830-43 engines as the previous variants, but beginning with the B-24G-10-NT production block, R-1830-65s were installed. The ball turret was also installed in the lower fuselage as a standard item beginning with this block.

The other noticeable change that first appeared on the B-24G concerned the nose gear doors. On previous variants, the nose gear doors moved upward to a position inside the well when the landing gear was extended. As a result, the doors were not visible when the gear was down. On the B-24G, the nose gear doors opened in a conventional manner along the sides of the well. Although some subsequent B-24Js would have the original doors that opened upward within the well, the B-24G marked the first time in Liberator production where the doors opened outward external of the nose gear well.

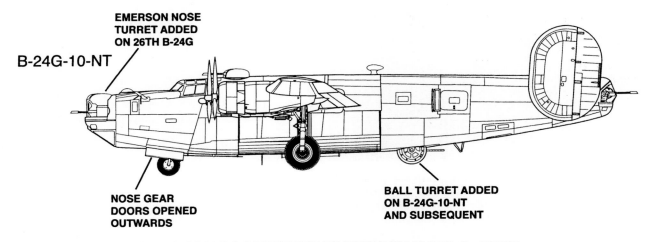

EMERSON NOSE TURRET ADDED ON 26TH B-24G

B-24G-10-NT

NOSE GEAR DOORS OPENED OUTWARDS

BALL TURRET ADDED ON B-24G-10-NT AND SUBSEQUENT

DETAIL & SCALE © COPYRIGHT DRAWING BY LLOYD S. JONES

B-24H

Like the B-24G, the B-24H had an Emerson turret in the nose. This Liberator is B-24H-1-CF, 42-64435, and it was built before the arrangement of the wing tip navigation lights was changed. (USAFM)

Compared to B-24D production numbers, relatively few B-24Es and B-24Gs were delivered. The next variant to be produced in large numbers was the B-24H, with a total of 3,100 being delivered from the Willow Run, Fort Worth, and Tulsa production lines. The B-24H was very similar to the B-24G, and the Emerson nose turret continued to be a standard feature. An improved Consolidated A-6B tail turret was also installed in the tail. The top turret was changed to a Martin A-3D "high hat" design that afforded the gunner much better visibility. The windows for the waist guns were enclosed with a clear glazing to improve crew comfort in the aft fuselage compart-

Details of the scanning window, external nose gear doors, and the pitot tube are revealed in this close-up of B-24H-15-CF, 41-29358. The fire extinguisher panel is red with white lettering. Also note the armor plate on the side of the cockpit to protect the pilot.

(Lloyd collection)

Compare the scanning window on B-24H-25-FO, 42-95283, to the one on the earlier B-24H-15-CF at left. Also note the additional bombardier's side window on the chin of the aircraft. These are examples of the many small differences found on Liberators of the same variant but produced at different plants. (Lloyd collection)

Some Liberators were equipped with various radar antennas to allow bombing in overcast conditions. B-24H-1-FO, 42-7644, is shown here in markings for the 66th Bomb Squadron of the 44th Bomb Group. It was attached to the 93rd Bomb Group, to serve as a pathfinder on a mission to Frankfurt on January 22, 1944. This was the first pathfinder mission. It has the original AN/APS-15 Mickey radar antenna in place of its ball turret. Subsequent models of the radar were smaller, and therefore their radome created less drag when extended. (Lloyd collection)

ment. However, the guns remained mounted in the center of the enclosed windows at the bottom.

B-24Hs, including the B-24H-DT, B-24H-1-CF, and B-24H-1-FO, had the R-1830-65 engines, but the remaining blocks were delivered with R-1830-43 powerplants.

Previous variants of the Liberator had two small navigation lights on each wing tip. One light was on top of each tip panel, and a second light was on the under-surface of each tip as illustrated on page 29. During B-24H production, these were replaced with a single light on the outer edge of each tip. Although some later ver-

sions of the Liberator would be delivered with the earlier arrangement, this marked the first appearance of the new light design on B-24s.

In the RAF, B-24Hs were called the Liberator VI, but this designation was shared with some B-24Js as well.

The Martin A-3D "high hat" turret replaced the lower design used on earlier variants. It provided the gunner with a much better field of view by allowing his head to be higher inside the dome. (Lloyd collection)

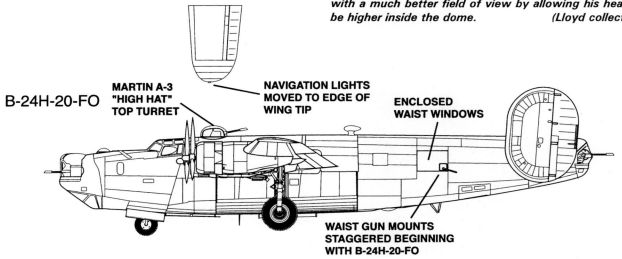

B-24H-20-FO

MARTIN A-3 "HIGH HAT" TOP TURRET

NAVIGATION LIGHTS MOVED TO EDGE OF WING TIP

ENCLOSED WAIST WINDOWS

WAIST GUN MOUNTS STAGGERED BEGINNING WITH B-24H-20-FO

DETAIL & SCALE © COPYRIGHT DRAWING BY LLOYD S. JONES

B-24J

Because of a shortage of Emerson turrets, most B-24Js were delivered with Consolidated turrets in the nose. Most of those produced in San Diego, like this B-24J-95-CO, did not have enclosed waist windows or the "high hat" dorsal turret. Note the whip antenna on the spine of this Liberator. (Lloyd collection)

Production of the B-24J exceeded that of any other Liberator variant with a total of 6,678 being built at San Diego, Willow Run, Fort Worth, Dallas, and Tulsa. Several minor, but noticeable, differences distinguished those produced by Consolidated at San Diego from those that were delivered from the other four plants.

The production of B-24Js far exceeded the availability of Emerson turrets, so Consolidated turrets were used in both nose and tail positions for most B-24Js regardless

The nose installation of the Consolidated turret is clearly visible on "I'LL BE AROUND." The nose gear doors are not visible, and this indicates that this B-24J was built by Consolidated in San Diego. (Lloyd collection)

of where they were produced. Late in the production run of the B-24J, the supply of Emerson turrets was sufficient to allow them to be installed in the nose position while the Consolidated turret remained the standard tail armament. The change to the Emerson nose turret was made with production blocks B-24J-190-CO and B-24J-45-CF on the San Diego and Fort Worth assembly lines respectively.

Except for the ones built at San Diego, B-24Js had enclosed and staggered waist gun positions. This feature was added late during production of B-24Js built at San Diego. It should be noted that the gun windows were not staggered as they were on late B-17Gs. On Liberators, it was the guns and their mounts that were staggered rather than the windows themselves. The left waist gun was mounted at the lower aft corner of the window, and the right waist gun was mounted at the lower front corner. This arrangement gave the gunners a little extra room as they aimed and fired their weapons.

Most B-24Js built at San Diego had the original nose gear doors which opened internally, and they retained the earlier dorsal turret with the low dome until the later production blocks. They also had the navigation lights on the top and bottom of each wing tip like those found on the early variants. All other B-24Js had the "high hat" top turret, the nose gear doors that opened externally, enclosed, staggered, waist windows, and the single navigation light mounted directly on the edge of each wing tip. Most of these features would be added to B-24Js built in San Diego as production continued. It was also during the B-24J production run that the scanning windows for the deleted tunnel gun were removed from the lower aft fuselage.

Features found on all B-24Js included R-1830-65 engines, an improved fuel system, a new M series bomb

sight, a C-1 automatic pilot, and electronic supercharger regulators. Beginning with the B-24J-210-CO production block, deicing boots were deleted from the wing and tail surfaces. These were replaced with a Thermal Ice Preventative System (TIPS) that used hot air from the engines to prevent ice buildup on the leading edges of the flying surfaces. All B-24J-NTs had the TIPS deicing system. A total of 172 B-24Js had antennas mounted in blisters under the nose for Ferret missions. Others had Mickey antenna domes in place of their ball turrets so they could serve as pathfinders on blind bombing missions.

Some B-24Js in the RAF were called Liberator VIs like the B-24H, while later production B-24Js were named Liberator VIIIs.

This B-24J-170-CO, 44-40559, illustrates how even late production B-24Js built by Consolidated at San Diego still had nose gear doors that opened internally and a Consolidated nose turret. These features were not changed to the external doors and the Emerson nose turret on the San Diego assembly line until the B-24J-190-CO production block. Also note the open waist windows. However, this aircraft does have the "high hat" dorsal turret and the single navigation light on the edge of each wing tip, both of which were added fairly late on the San Diego B-24J production line. The scanning windows for the tunnel gun have also been deleted from the lower aft fuselage. (Lloyd collection)

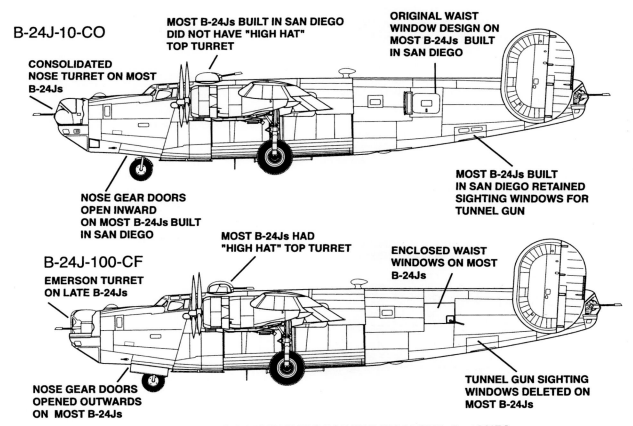

B-24J-10-CO

CONSOLIDATED NOSE TURRET ON MOST B-24Js

MOST B-24Js BUILT IN SAN DIEGO DID NOT HAVE "HIGH HAT" TOP TURRET

ORIGINAL WAIST WINDOW DESIGN ON MOST B-24Js BUILT IN SAN DIEGO

NOSE GEAR DOORS OPEN INWARD ON MOST B-24Js BUILT IN SAN DIEGO

MOST B-24Js BUILT IN SAN DIEGO RETAINED SIGHTING WINDOWS FOR TUNNEL GUN

B-24J-100-CF

EMERSON TURRET ON LATE B-24Js

MOST B-24Js HAD "HIGH HAT" TOP TURRET

ENCLOSED WAIST WINDOWS ON MOST B-24Js

NOSE GEAR DOORS OPENED OUTWARDS ON MOST B-24Js

TUNNEL GUN SIGHTING WINDOWS DELETED ON MOST B-24Js

DETAIL & SCALE © COPYRIGHT DRAWING BY LLOYD S. JONES

55

B-24L

The B-24L was a lightweight version of the Liberator. B-24L-15-FO, 44-49946, was one of several B-24Ls modified to train B-29 crew members. All armament was removed, and the turret positions were covered with sheet metal. These aircraft were redesignated RB-24Ls, but this was subsequently changed to TB-24L.
(Lloyd collection)

Although it was basically similar to the B-24J in most respects, the B-24L was an attempt to produce a lighter version of the Liberator. The 1,667 B-24Ls were over 1,000 pounds lighter than the previous B-24J. This weight savings was accomplished mainly by deleting the tail and ball turrets. With long range fighter escorts becoming available in large numbers, it was believed that the bombers did not have to be as heavily armed.

In place of the Consolidated turret in the tail, an M-6A machine gun mount was installed. Called the "stinger," this mount contained two .50-caliber machine guns, but it was manually operated through a large clear glazing. This was sometimes replaced with different armaments at depots in the various theaters depending on operation needs. The enclosed stinger mount was sometimes replaced with an open twin-gun arrangement, while other B-24Ls had standard A-6B Consolidated power-operated turrets installed at the field depots.

B-24Ls were built at Willow Run and San Diego, and the staggered, enclosed, waist gun positions finally became a production standard on all B-24Ls in San Diego. This feature had long been used on Liberators built on the other production lines. B-24Ls also had large rectangular scanning windows in the nose to provide better visibility for the navigator and bombardier.

Several B-24Ls were converted to RB-24Ls and were used to train B-29 aircrews. No armament was carried, and the nose and tail positions were covered over with sheet metal fairings. These Liberators were subsequently redesignated TB-24Ls. One B-24L was also converted to the XB-24Q and used by Boeing to test a radar-controlled gun turret.

Many B-24Ls were fitted with a manually operated M-6A "stinger" gun mount in the tail. This unit was much lighter than the powered Consolidated turret, and its installation was one of the measures initially taken to reduce the weight of the B-24L. *(Lloyd collection)*

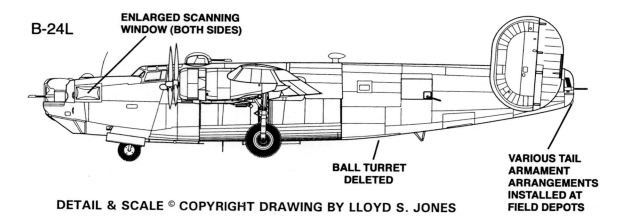

B-24L

ENLARGED SCANNING WINDOW (BOTH SIDES)

BALL TURRET DELETED

VARIOUS TAIL ARMAMENT ARRANGEMENTS INSTALLED AT FIELD DEPOTS

DETAIL & SCALE © COPYRIGHT DRAWING BY LLOYD S. JONES

Above: In the post-war years, some C-87s were obtained by civilians. "The Explorer" was owned by Milton Reynolds and flown to China on an expedition for the Boston Museum. The pilot's name, Capt. W. P. Odom, is painted above the two aft windows on the side of the fuselage.

(Lloyd collection)

Right: The interior of the C-87 had seating for twenty passengers. The seats could be removed to carry up to 12,000 pounds of cargo.

(Lloyd collection)

C-87-CF

ALL TURRETS DELETED

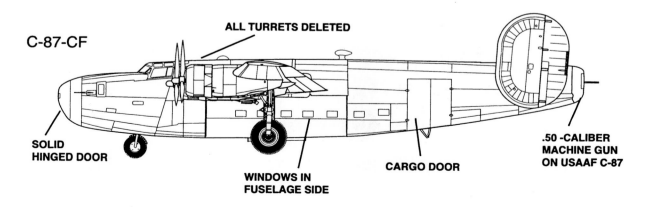

SOLID HINGED DOOR

WINDOWS IN FUSELAGE SIDE

CARGO DOOR

.50 -CALIBER MACHINE GUN ON USAAF C-87

DETAIL & SCALE © COPYRIGHT DRAWING BY LLOYD S. JONES

F-7 PHOTO RECONNAISSANCE LIBERATORS

F-7A, 42-64051, was assigned to the 20th Combat Mapping Squadron of the 6th Photo Group. This unit was part of the 5th Air Force. Dark touch-up paint has been sprayed around the camera window on the right side of the nose.
(Lloyd collection)

The concept of developing a long range photographic reconnaissance version of the Liberator began when a single B-24D airframe was converted to the XF-7 with eleven cameras installed in the nose, bomb bay, and aft fuselage section. This experimental aircraft was followed by four B-24Ds which were similarly modified to F-7 standards by the Northwest Modification Center at St. Paul, Minnesota.

The F-7A was the first Liberator reconnaissance version to be converted in larger numbers with eighty-nine being modified from B-24J airframes. They carried a trimetregon camera in the nose and two vertical cameras in the aft bomb bay.

The final photo recon variant of the Liberator was the F-7B, 124 of which were converted from 122 B-24J and two B-24M airframes. These had five cameras, all of which were carried in the bomb bay.

F-7A

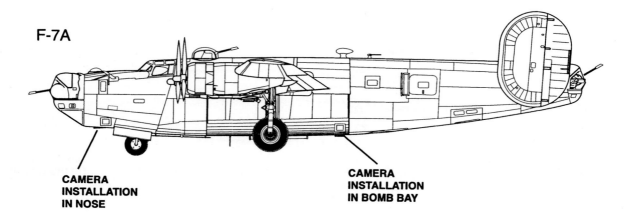

**CAMERA
INSTALLATION
IN NOSE**

**CAMERA
INSTALLATION
IN BOMB BAY**

DETAIL & SCALE © COPYRIGHT DRAWING BY LLOYD S. JONES

C-109 TANKER & C-31 LIBERATOR LINER

Above: After a single XC-109 was converted from a B-24E, 208 C-109 tankers were modified from B-24J and B-24Ls. All armament was removed, and extra fuel tanks were installed inside the nose, bomb bay and aft fuselage, bringing the total fuel capacity to 2,400 gallons. Most C-109s were used in the China-India-Burma Theater where they transported fuel over "The Hump" to support air operations. Here, C-109, 44-48879, takes on fuel. This tanker was assigned to the 2nd Air Transport Squadron. Although they were referred to as tankers, the C-109s were actually fuel transports. They did not supply fuel directly to other aircraft like present-day tankers do.
(Lloyd collection)

Below: Consolidated built two Liberator Liners using standard B-24 wings, the single PB4Y-2 vertical tail, and an entirely new fuselage that could carry 104 passengers. They were powered by R-1830-94 engines and were called Model 39 by Consolidated. The first airframe was planned for use by the Navy and designated the R2Y. One was sold to American Airlines, but no orders were placed for an airliner version. One of the Liberator Liners is shown here at LaGuardia Field, New York, in standard company markings. The stripes on the tail are blue and white, while the markings on the fuselage and engine cowlings are red and white. LIBERATOR EXPRESS is lettered in white with a blue outline. (Piet collection)

PB4Y-1

The first PB4Y-1s were simply B-24Ds taken from USAAF deliveries, but the Navy soon started adding modifications to improve the Liberators for their specific requirements. Many early PB4Y-1s had the standard B-24D nose glazing as shown here, but like their USAAF counterparts, some had Consolidated, Emerson, or ERCO turrets added in the bow. *(National Archives)*

PB4Y-1, *and the bureau number, 31936, have been stenciled above the USAAF serial number on this B-24D as it is prepared to be delivered to the Navy. Although the early PB4Y-1s were originally painted in the standard USAAF Olive Drab over Neutral Gray scheme, they were soon repainted in the Navy's blue and white camouflage.* *(National Archives)*

When the United States entered World War II, the USAAF flew the long range anti-submarine warfare (ASW) patrols extending out from America's coastlines. In mid-1942, the Navy began flying these patrols, and by late 1943, this task was completely discontinued by the USAAF, leaving it the sole responsibility of the Navy.

Although the Navy was using Lockheed PBO Hudsons, PV-1 Venturas, and PV-2 Harpoons, and North American B-25 Mitchells (redesignated PBJ by the Navy) to perform these duties, it needed aircraft with longer range to reach out further from the shore to protect convoys and other shipping. Thirty-one B-17s (called PB-1s in Navy service) were acquired, but the B-24's airframe was far better suited for these patrol missions. As a result, existing B-24Ds were turned over to the Navy and redesignated PB4Y-1s. But even though the designation was changed, the Navy continued to use the name Liberator for the aircraft. These original PB4Y-1s were continually supplemented by additional deliveries from B-24Ds already on order by the Army, and a total of 977 PB4Y-1 Liberators would eventually be acquired by the Navy. The first PB4Y-1s entered service when VP-101 became operational at NAS Barbers Point, Hawaii, in September 1942.

The Navy added Engineering and Research Company (ERCO) bow turrets to some of the original B-24Ds it received, and later Liberators, delivered off the production lines to the Navy as PB4Y-1s, had Consolidated or Emerson bow turrets. The Navy also sometimes replaced the ball turrets with a retractable search radar dome. As the Liberator design was improved, PB4Y-1s continued to be delivered from B-24J, B-24L, and B-24M production blocks coming from Consolidated's San Diego plant. They included the same improvements made to the B-24s including the enclosed and staggered waist windows.

PB4Y-1s continued in service with the Navy after World War II, and five were operated by the Coast Guard for search and rescue duties from 1944 through 1946. In 1952, PB4Y-1s remaining in service had cameras added to perform photographic reconnaissance missions, and these aircraft were redesignated PB4Y-1Ps.

Above: This PB4Y-1 has the spherical ERCO turret in the bow. This turret was added to a number of early PB4Y-1s at field depots, but some Consolidated turrets and even a few Emerson turrets were installed in the bows of other PB4Y-1s.
(Jones collection)

Right: In the post-war years, many PB4Y-1s remained in service with the Navy. In 1952, they had cameras added and were redesignated PB4Y-1Ps for the photographic reconnaissance mission. *(NMNA)*

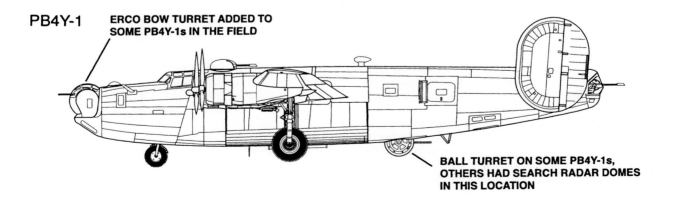

PB4Y-1   **ERCO BOW TURRET ADDED TO SOME PB4Y-1s IN THE FIELD**

BALL TURRET ON SOME PB4Y-1s, OTHERS HAD SEARCH RADAR DOMES IN THIS LOCATION

DETAIL & SCALE © COPYRIGHT DRAWING BY LLOYD S. JONES

PB4Y-2 PRIVATEER

The PB4Y-2 Privateer was a significantly redesigned version of the B-24 airframe that was optimized for long range patrols at low altitudes. Often operating alone and unescorted, it relied on its six power-operated turrets for defense. This included two Martin turrets on top of the fuselage. (Lloyd collection)

Although the PB4Y-1 was excellent for long range patrol missions, it was still basically a land bomber. The Navy wanted to optimize the design specifically for patrol duties, and the PB4Y-2 Privateer was developed. Because patrol missions were flown almost exclusively at low altitudes, the turbosuperchargers were deleted from the R-1830-94 engines. A single vertical tail design, previously used on the B-24K, was chosen to provide better stability.

The fuselage was lengthened a total of seven feet to make room for additional crew members and to add a second Martin A-3D dorsal turret. A flight engineer's station and a special operations station, manned by a radar operator, were added. The flight engineer and radar operator, along with the gunner for the second dorsal turret, were the additional crew members assigned to the Privateer.

Patrol aircraft usually flew without the benefit of a fighter escort, so adequate defensive armament was essential. In addition to the second top turret, the Navy specified power operated turrets in the nose, tail, and both waist positions. A total of twelve .50-caliber machine guns were carried in the six turrets. Most unusual of these were the two ERCO turrets in the waist position. These large blisters could cover a much wider field of fire with their twin machine guns than could the standard waist positions in B-24s. The guns could be depressed downward past the ninety-degree vertical to overlap their fire and cover the area directly below the aircraft, so there was no need for the ball turret in the lower fuselage. Most Privateers had an ERCO ball turret in the bow and a lightweight Consolidated A-6B turret in the tail, but photographic evidence indicates that some had the Consolidated turrets in both positions.

A series of antennas was located under the nose and elsewhere on the skin of the PB4Y-2. Most of these were for electronic countermeasures (ECM) gear including the AN/APR-1, AN/APR-2, and AN/APR-5 radar intercept receivers and AN/ARR-5 communications intercept receivers. Jammers included the AN/APT-1, AN/APT-5, and AN/APQ-2 systems. Not all equipment was carried all of the time. Instead, it was selected based on what was required for the specific mission being flown. With this wide variety of equipment available, PB4Y-2s flew radio relay and barrier support missions for the fleet, in addition to performing their normal patrol duties. Some were also employed using the SWOD-9 Bat anti-shipping missiles.

With all these changes, the new aircraft was considerably different from the standard Liberator, so the Navy changed the name to Privateer in the tradition of small ships that patrolled the oceans in earlier times.

Three B-24Ds were converted to XPB4Y-2 evaluation aircraft, and these were followed by 736 production PB4Y-2s, all of which were built by Consolidated at San Diego. Sixty-one were lost during World War II due to all causes. The survivors served throughout the remainder of World War II and for many years thereafter including three squadrons that saw action in Korea. Nine were transferred to the U. S. Coast Guard while others were provided to the French, Nationalist Chinese, and the Hondurans.

A transport version, designated the RY-3, was also developed, and thirty-nine were completed. They were originally built for the RAF, but only one was sent to Britain, with the other thirty-eight being retained by the U. S. Navy. Twenty-seven Liberator IXs, which were

Although most PB4Y-2s had ERCO bow turrets like the one shown in the photograph above, this Privateer has a Consolidated A-6 turret in its bow. (National Archives)

An underside view shows additional details of the PB4Y-2. Note the lack of turbosuperchargers on the engines as found on B-24s. *(Lloyd collection)*

also based on the RY-3 design, were delivered to the Royal Air Force.

In the post-war years, some Privateers were modified to carry ASM-N-2 anti-shipping missiles. These were redesignated PB4Y-2Bs, but they were also known as PB4Y-2Ms. The PB4Y-2S version had a surface search radar, and nine Privateers transferred to the Coast Guard were designated PB4Y-2Gs. These were used for air-sea rescue and weather reconnaissance missions. PB4Y-2Ks, later redesignated QP-4Bs, were used by the Navy as radio controlled drones.

On September 1, 1962, the bomber mission was dropped, and the few remaining Privateers in the Navy were redesignated P-4Bs. The last ones in U. S. service were flown by the Coast Guard until the mid-1960s. In Navy service, the Privateers were replaced with the P-3 Orion, and this aircraft remains the Navy's only long range, land based patrol aircraft to this day.

A close-up shows the numerous antenna fairings under the nose for some of the electronic gear. *(NMNA)*

Above: The transport version of the Privateer was designated the RY-3 by the Navy. *(Piet collection)*

Right: The final Privateers in service with the United States were flown by the Coast Guard for search and rescue missions until the mid-1960s. The right landing gear collapsed on this Coast Guard Privateer as it made its landing. This resulted in a ground loop, but there was relatively little damage to the aircraft. *(NMNA)*

PB4Y-2 PRIVATEER DIMENSION DRAWINGS

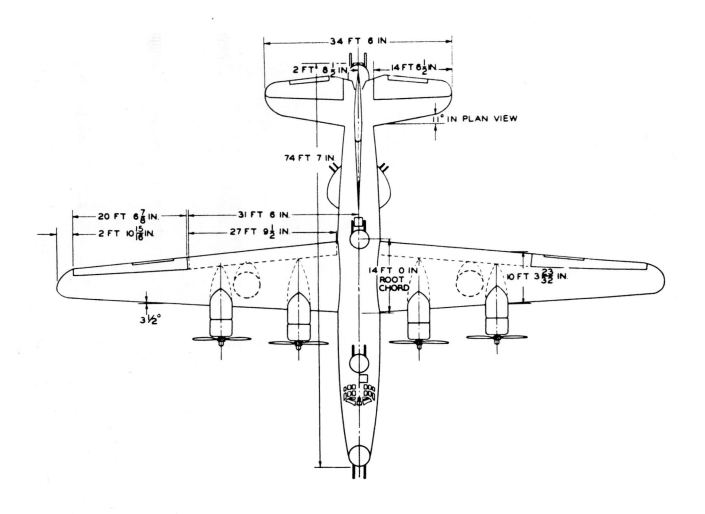

34 FT 6 IN

2 FT 8½ IN · 14 FT 6½ IN

11° IN PLAN VIEW

74 FT 7 IN

20 FT 6⅞ IN. · 31 FT 6 IN.

2 FT 10¹⁵⁄₁₆ IN. · 27 FT 9½ IN.

14 FT 0 IN ROOT CHORD · 10 FT 3²³⁄₃₂ IN.

3½°

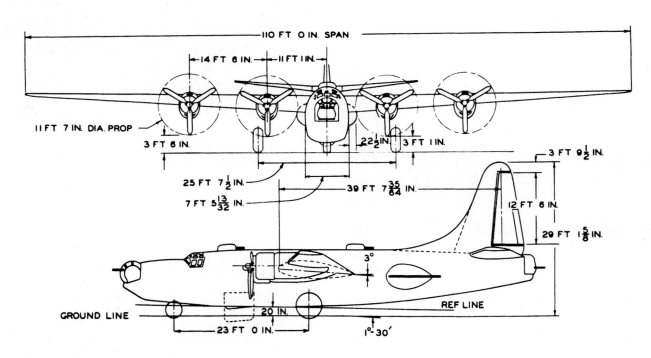

110 FT 0 IN. SPAN

14 FT 6 IN. · 11 FT 1 IN.

11 FT 7 IN. DIA. PROP

3 FT 6 IN. · 22½ IN. · 3 FT 1 IN.

3 FT 9½ IN.

25 FT 7½ IN. · 39 FT 7³⁵⁄₆₄ IN.

12 FT 6 IN.

7 FT 5¹³⁄₃₂ IN.

29 FT 1⅝ IN.

3°

GROUND LINE · 20 IN. · REF LINE

23 FT 0 IN. · 1°-30'

68

PB4Y-2 PRIVATEER DETAILS

COCKPIT DETAILS

Although the basic arrangement of the instrument panel in the PB4Y-2 was very similar to that found in the B-24, the layout and number of instruments differed to some extent. *(National Archives)*

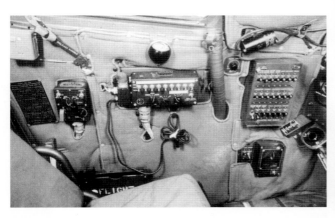

The sides of the cockpit were covered with heavy cloth panels that snapped into place. Controls for the intercom and a circuit breaker panel can be seen on the pilot's side. *(National Archives)*

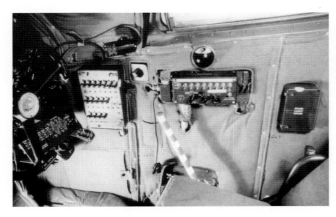

The co-pilot's side also had switches for the intercom system and additional circuit breakers. Compare the photographs on this page with the photographs of the B-24D's cockpit on pages 18 and 19. *(National Archives)*

This view looks up and forward at the series of overhead panels in the center of the cockpit. *(National Archives)*

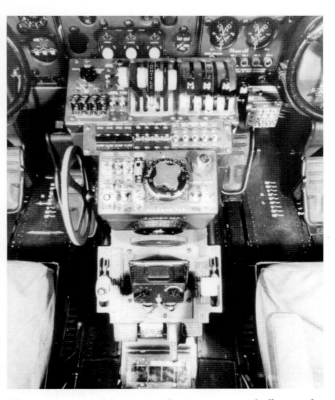

The center stand between the seats was similar to the one in B-24s, but a noticeable difference was the lack of handles for the supercharger controls. The Privateer had no superchargers on its engines. *(National Archives)*

NOSE COMPARTMENT INTERIOR DETAILS

This view looks forward in the bombardier's compartment, and the bomb aiming window and two side windows can be seen in the background. A pad was provided for the bombardier to kneel on as he sighted through the window, and a sling supported his upper body. (National Archives)

These panels were on the left side of the bombardier's compartment near the front. At the top is a small panel with an altimeter and an air speed indicator. The bombs that were to be released were selected on the large panel at the center, and the lower panel controlled the bomb release sequence. (National Archives)

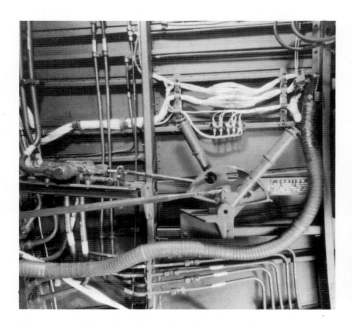

The manual bomb release handles were located further aft on the left side of the bombardier's compartment. (National Archives)

Generators were located in the nose compartment. To the right is the crawlway leading forward to the bombardier's compartment. (National Archives)

FORWARD FUSELAGE INTERIOR DETAILS

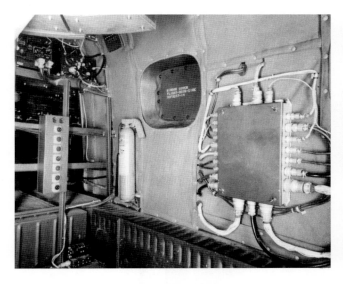

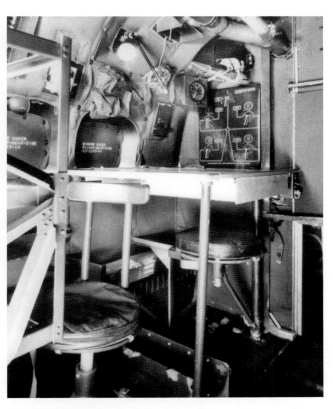

Above left: This view looks aft and to the left side of the fuselage directly behind the cockpit. The rack for the radio gear can be seen to the left. Again, note the snap-in heavy cloth panels around the equipment.
(National Archives)

Above right: The navigator's station was located on the right side of the fuselage. *(National Archives)*

The radio operator's station was on the left side in the forward fuselage compartment. The various radios were installed in a rack above the table. *(National Archives)*

A radar operator sat at the special operations station. He was responsible for all of the aircraft's radar and electronic countermeasures systems. *(National Archives)*

DITCHING HAMMOCKS

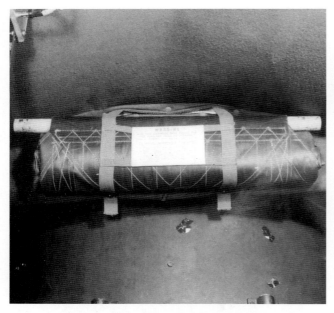

Because the Privateer spent a lot of time flying over water, ditching hammocks were provided for the crew members. This is the forward hammock shown in the stowed position. *(National Archives)*

In this view, taken through the top hatch, three Consolidated employees are shown demonstrating the correct position for ditching on the erected forward ditching hammock. *(National Archives)*

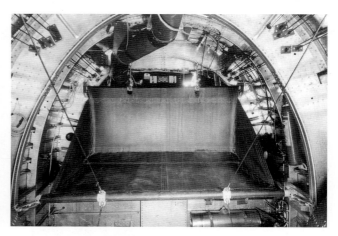

In this view, the hammock in the aft fuselage compartment is shown ready for use in the erected position. *(National Archives)*

Above: The ditching hammock for the crewmembers in the aft fuselage was located at the forward end of the compartment where the wing structure strengthened the fuselage. *(National Archives)*

Right: The hammock was deep enough to accommodate seven people in the ditching position. *(National Archives)*

AFT FUSELAGE INTERIOR DETAILS

Above left: The toilet was nothing more than a covered can mounted on the floor near the side of the fuselage. Note the empty toilet paper holder on the half bulkhead next to the toilet. (National Archives)

Above right: The interior of the aft fuselage compartment was usually an unpainted natural metal. Stringers, hydraulic plumbing, and control lines are visible around the sides and overhead. Also note that the floor is simply slats in the center of the fuselage. Ammunition boxes for the waist turrets are visible in the foreground of this view that looks forward. (National Archives)

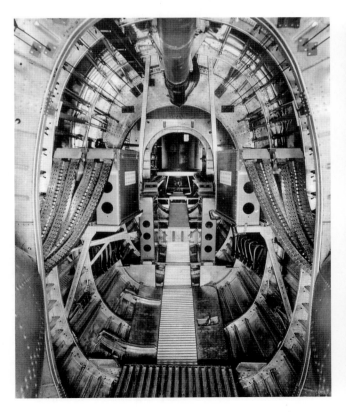

This photograph looks toward the rear from a point even with the waist turrets. The metal belts that fed ammunition to the waist gun turrets are visible on each side of the fuselage. (National Archives)

At the end of the aft fuselage compartment was the rear turret. Note the ammunition belts that extend along the sides of the fuselage, then enter the turret from below. (National Archives)

POWERPLANT DETAILS

The PB4Y-2 Privateer was powered by R-1830-94 engines which did not have turbosuperchargers. Instead of having scoops on each side of the cowl ring like the B-24 did, the scoops were located at the top and bottom. However, in this photograph, the top scoops do not show up because of the dark shadows. Also note the shape of the propeller blades. These were a slightly different shape than those used on Liberators and were optimized to be efficient at lower altitudes where the PB4Y-2 was designed to operate. In some cases, the tips of the propellers on Navy aircraft were not painted yellow.
(National Archives)

Panels have been removed from the cowling on the left outboard (Number 1) engine to reveal details inside. Note how the exhaust vents on the inside surface of the nacelle. This arrangement was used on the two outboard engines. (National Archives)

On the two inboard powerplants, the exhausts were routed further aft to a location low on the centerline of the nacelle. This photograph shows details on the inboard side of the left inboard (Number 2) engine.
(National Archives)

In this view, taken behind the right inboard (Number 3) engine, the exhaust port under the nacelle is clearly visible. Just forward of the exhaust port is a large vent for the oil cooler's radiator. (National Archives)

Details on the inboard side of the right outboard (Number 4) engine are revealed here. Much of the aft end of the nacelle was simply an empty aerodynamic fairing.
(National Archives)

The top and bottom scoops in the cowl ring were not the same size as the two side scoops used on the B-24. The bottom scoop was much larger. (National Archives)

A Consolidated employee turns the hand crank on the left side of the left inboard engine on a PB4Y-2. (National Archives)

Details on the aft end of the R-1830-94 powerplant are shown here. This is the installation for the left outboard engine. (National Archives)

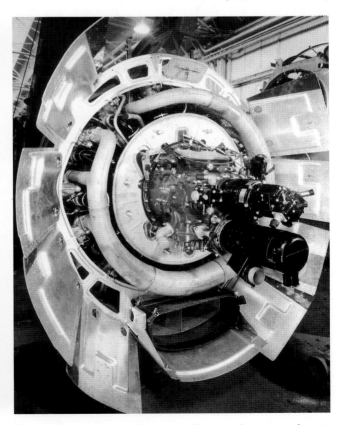

The arrangement of the cowl flaps, exhaust, and vent indicate that this is the right outboard engine. (National Archives)

WAIST BLISTER GUN TURRET DETAILS

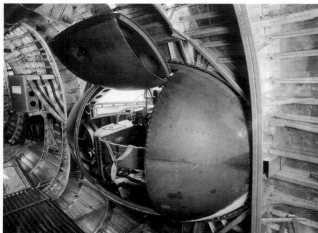

Above left: An ERCO waist turret is being installed on the right side of a PB4Y-2. The top area of the blister above the guns was clear glazing, while the lower section was solid. (National Archives)

Above right: An installed and painted ERCO waist turret is shown here on the left side of the fuselage. The blistered turret doubled the firepower and provided a field of fire that was considerably greater than the standard waist guns used on the B-24. (National Archives)

Left: An overall view of the left waist turret shows how the folding doors provided access for the gunner. (National Archives)

This close-up looks toward the rear inside the left waist turret. Details of the seat and sight are revealed. Visibility from the blister was excellent. (National Archives)

Part of the hydraulic system that operated the turret in elevation is visible in this view that looks forward into the left waist turret blister. (National Archives)

TAIL DETAILS

Above: The shape of the vertical tail is revealed in a direct side view. Note that the actuator for the trim tab on the rudder is on the right side. (National Archives)

Below: From directly behind the aircraft, the amount of dihedral on the horizontal tails is apparent. On B-24s with twin vertical tails, the horizontal tail had no dihedral. (National Archives)

The large rudder covered over three-fourths of the height of the vertical tail, and three large hinges connected it to the vertical stabilizer. A large trim tab was at its base. Details of the lightweight Consolidated tail turret are also visible in this view. (National Archives)

MODELERS SUMMARY

Note: Each volume in Detail & Scale's "In Detail" Series of publications has a Modelers Summary in the back of the book. The Modelers Summary will discuss the injection-molded plastic model kits of the aircraft covered by the book, and all common modeling scales from 1/144th through 1/32nd scale will be included. Highlights of the better kits in each scale will be discussed, and recommendations will be made with respect to which kit or kits in each scale are the best for the serious scale modeler to use. Once a kit has been purchased, the modeler should compare the various features of the kit to the drawings and photographs in the book to determine how accurately and extensively they are represented. He can then decide what, if any, correcting or detailing work he wants to do to enhance the appearance of the model.

GENERAL COMMENTS

Injection-molded plastic model kits are available of the Liberator in the standard 1/144th, 1/72nd, and 1/48th modeling scales. Because of the many differences in details between one version and the next, and even within the same variant depending on which plant produced it, Detail & Scale cautions modelers to get the most detailed reference material possible. The best situation is to have an actual photograph of the Liberator to be modeled, and check such features as scanning windows, types of turrets used, waist windows, the bombardier's windows, and the arrangement of navigation lights on the wings. In all likelihood, it will be necessary to make some modifications regardless of what kit is used.

1/144th SCALE KITS

Crown, Revell, and Minicraft have released 1/144th scale kits of the Liberator, but all are actually the same moldings released under different labels. The only differences are the box art, instructions, and decals.

The features of the model most closely represent a B-24J from Consolidated's San Diego facility. It has the Consolidated turrets in both the nose and tail positions, but the top turret more closely represents the "high hat" design than the one with the original lower dome. The nose gear doors are the ones that open externally, but these are easily left off if they are not appropriate for the particular Liberator being modeled. The waist gun positions are the original open design, but they are depicted with the covers in place. The small windows in the covers, as well as the scanning windows for the tunnel gun in the lower aft fuselage, are simply scribed into the plastic. All windows can be opened up and filled with Krystal Klear or small pieces of clear plastic. Many B-24Js had the scanning windows for the tunnel gun deleted, so these can be sanded off if necessary. Other small windows in the fuselage are also represented only by scribed lines, so these need to be opened up and filled with either Krystal Klear or clear plastic. Most important of these are the scanning windows in the nose, but be sure to choose the correct design for the Liberator being modeled.

Detailing is not particularly good. There are no representations of the cylinders inside the nacelles, and neither arrangement of wing navigation lights is represented on the wing tips. The turbosuperchargers are likewise very simple, and only a floor with two seats is included for the cockpit.

The shape of the propeller blades is incorrect, being a bit too broad near the hubs. The canopy also has some shape problems, being too sloped on top. Otherwise the shapes and outlines are generally correct. We would rate this kit as being about average in 1/144th scale. It is neither outstanding nor particularly poor.

The Cobra Company has two conversion kits for this model. One is for the B-24D and the other is for a PB4Y-1. Both provide parts for the entire forward fuselage including the cockpit and canopy, and both provide detailed engines. The PB4Y-1 comes with the ERCO bow turret, while the B-24D has the standard nose glazing. Each enhances the basic 1/144th scale Liberator model.

The Cobra Company also has a complete resin kit of the PB4Y-2 Privateer with a retail price of $60.00. White metal landing gear, vacu-formed clear parts, and etched metal flaps, landing gear doors, tail skid, propeller blades, main instrument panel, and control wheels are included in this highly detailed 1/144th scale kit. The panel detailing is the recessed variety, and is nicely done.

The kit is very accurate, with one exception. The section between the bombardier's station and the bottom of the ERCO bow turret is very narrow on the actual aircraft. But on the kit, it is identical to that of the Crown/Revell/Minicraft plastic kit. This is correct for a B-24H through B-24M, but not for the PB4Y-2. The area of the nose around the turret has a downward sweep which is not represented in the kit. This is puzzling, because the drawings on the instruction sheet clearly show the correct shape. Nevertheless, we recommend this kit. It can be custom ordered from the Cobra Company at 3313 Pathway Court, Falls Church, Virginia 22042. Their phone number is (703) 204-9412.

1/72nd SCALE KITS

The oldest of the 1/72nd scale Liberator models is from Airfix, but it has also been released under the US Airfix, MPC, and Craft Master labels. It is crude, inaccurate, and it lacks detailing. It is covered with rivets, and surface detailing is poor. In short, it cannot be considered by a serious scale modeler.

The Revell 1/72nd scale Liberator, which has also been released as a PB4Y-1, is almost as old as the Airfix kit. It is more accurate than the Airfix model, but it too is covered with rivets. With the much better Minicraft kits available, we cannot recommend the Revell model.

Clearly, the best Liberator models in 1/72nd scale are the ones from Minicraft. Kits of the B-24D, B-24H, B-24J, B-24M, and PB4Y-1 have been released, and all are the same except for the necessary parts to represent the differences between the variants.

All of the kits have reasonably detailed and accurate interiors. This includes the bomb bays which have racks with bombs. The bomb bay doors can be assembled in the open or closed position.

One problem with all of the kits is that the turrets

The Minicraft 1/72nd scale B-24H was used by Bob Bartolacci to build this Liberator from the 834th Bomb Squadron of the 486th Bomb Group. These are the markings that come in the kit. **(Bartolacci)**

were molded in front and rear halves. This results in inaccuracies, and we recommend using replacement Consolidated turrets available from Squadron Products. Unfortunately, no replacement is available for the Emerson turret. Squadron Products also makes replacement clear parts for all Minicraft Liberators except the B-24M, and they are more accurate than those that come in the kits.

The kits with the enclosed waist windows have a minor inaccuracy in that the corners are slightly rounded instead of having the sharp ninety-degree angle. Window arrangements and the area between the forward turret and the nose section most closely depict a Liberator built by Ford in the B-24H, B-24J, and B-24M kits. But by modifying the windows and other features as necessary, the average modeler can complete the kits to represent any Liberator aircraft. The B-24H, B-24J, and B-24M kits have the Emerson and Consolidated nose turrets, so the correct one can be chosen for the aircraft being modeled.

The PB4Y-1 has a different lower panel with a retractable radome in place of the ball turret. A new forward fuselage section is provided along with an ERCO bow turret. The nose section has the small scanning windows found on PB4Y-1s that were converted from B-24Ds, but later PB4Y-1s had larger windows like those found on Privateers. The ERCO turret has two long protrusions extending from the upper clear section. These should be removed before the guns are added.

The first Privateer kit in 1/72nd scale was from Sutcliffe in England. This vacu-formed model was based on the Airfix B-24J, and it had numerous inaccuracies. The second 1/72nd scale Privateer model, and the only injection-molded kit issued to date, is from Matchbox. It offers optional parts to build a PB4Y-2, RY-3, or Churchill's personal aircraft named *Commando*.

The Matchbox kit is so crude and inaccurate that it simply cannot be used to build a Privateer model that even comes close to correctly representing the real thing. Shapes and outlines are inaccurate from nose to tail, and moldings are heavy, thick, and rough. It would be far better to use a Minicraft PB4Y-1 as the basis for a conversion. Start by stretching the fuselage, then use the vertical tail, horizontal tail, waist turret blisters, engine nacelles, and radar pods from the Matchbox kit. Squad-

ron Products makes the clear parts for the ERCO nose and waist turrets. Although it will take a lot of work, this conversion will result in a far more accurate model of the Privateer than simply using the Matchbox kit.

1/48th SCALE KITS

The only 1/48th scale Liberator model was originally released by Monogram in 1976. It has been reissued a number of times as both a B-24D and B-24J, and by the merged Revell-Monogram company as a B-24D in their Pro-Modeler line. The B-24J kit has the ball turret, while the B-24D kits do not.

All issues are very accurate and well detailed including the bomb bay, but the Pro-Modeler release has additional detailing including etched metal parts. The main problem with all issues involves the turrets which were molded with front and rear sections, and this causes some inaccuracies as in the Minicraft kits. To correct this, Koster Aero Enterprises produced a set of replacement turrets and a PB4Y-1 conversion kit for the Monogram Liberator. It provides both Consolidated and Emerson turrets with accurate seam lines. A new nose section, correct for the B-24H and B-24J, is included as is a ball turret. These Koster kits allow conversion of the B-24D model into a B-24H, B-24J, or PB4Y-1.

A more recent release from Koster is a PB4Y-2 Privateer conversion kit to be used with the Monogram 1/48th scale Liberator. It has front and rear fuselage sections including the single vertical tail design. Resin parts are included for all of the turrets. The different cowl rings, with the scoops at the top and bottom, are also in the kit, and the instructions explain how to modify the propeller blades to make them more accurately depict those used on the Privateer. A separate kit of white metal blades is also available from Koster.

The Monogram kit is excellent, but at the very least, the modeler should use the Koster turrets to replace those provided by Monogram. Except for the turrets, a very good model can be built right from the box.

The Monogram 1/48th scale B-24D was used by Stan Parker to build this Liberator III. It has markings for the 10th Bomber Reconnaissance Squadron of the Royal Canadian Air Force. **(Parker)**

More In Detail Titles from squadron/signal publications....

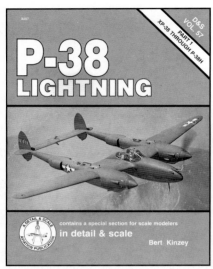

8257 P-38 Lightning Part 1

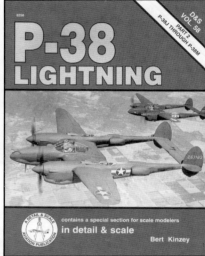

8258 P-38 Lightning Part 2

8259 F-84 Thunderjet

8261 P-40 Warhawk Part 1

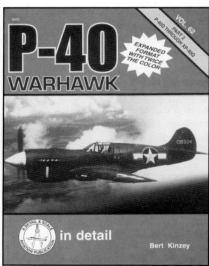

8262 P-40 Warhawk Part 2

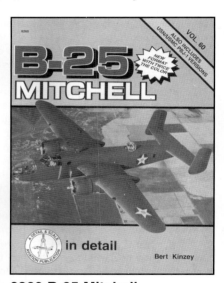

8260 B-25 Mitchell

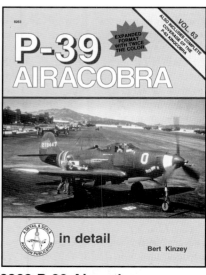

8263 P-39 Airacobra